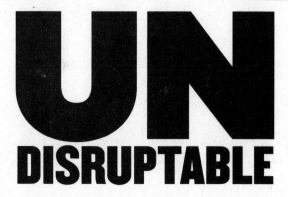

UN
DISRUPTABLE

Ian Whitworth is a Sydney entrepreneur who is testament to the fact that any fool can do it. Failed vet student, amusement ride operator, audiovisual technician, he had to start his own advertising agency so he could give himself the creative director job he yearned for. It won some awards, though, and helped him start audiovisual business Scene Change, partly to test marketing ideas that his corporate clients felt were too weird. It worked, becoming a successful national firm in the event industry, a sector smashed worse than most by COVID-19. Ian's blog, 'Motivation For Sceptics', provides an honest and darkly amusing window into the reality of entrepreneur life. His writing also appears in the *Sydney Morning Herald*, *The Age* and *Smart Company*.

ianwhitworth.net

To Erica, Don and Val: lifelong inspirations.

TIMELESS BUSINESS
TRUTHS FOR THRIVING
IN A WORLD OF
NON-STOP CHANGE

UN
DISRUPTABLE

IAN WHITWORTH

LIFE

PENGUIN LIFE
UK | USA | Canada | Ireland | Australia
India | New Zealand | South Africa | China

Penguin Life is part of the Penguin Random House group of companies whose
addresses can be found at global.penguinrandomhouse.com

Penguin
Random House
Australia

First published by Penguin Life in 2021

Cover background by Ivan Kovbasniuk/Shutterstock
Cover design by Alex Ross © Penguin Random House Australia Pty Ltd
Internal design by Alex Ross
Typeset in 11/15pt Berkley Book by Midland Typesetters, Australia

Printed and bound in Australia by Griffin Press, part of Ovato, an accredited
ISO AS/NZS 14001 Environmental Management Systems printer

A catalogue record for this
book is available from the
National Library of Australia

ISBN 978 1 76104 219 5

penguin.com.au

CONTENTS

Contents

I.

TAKE SOME CONTROL OVER YOUR LIFE

GET YOUR TICKET
OUT OF THERE

Business. Read the textbooks and you're in no doubt that it's a sensible career of deep dullness. A maze of charts, checklists and uninteresting plans 'going forward', piled up late into the evening while all your friends are pro streamers, resort reviewers or kombucha sommeliers. Or so their social media feeds tell you, when you take a break from writing your quarterly report on hose nozzle pricing.

The books don't do it justice. Business is more fun than monkey butlers. If you choose to make it so. *Owning* a business, that is. Sure, it's a ton of work, but it's also the complete design-your-own-reality experience. It's the only field where people who are not particularly good looking, have no sports or entertainment talent and aren't as smart as scientists can create their own world where they can do as they please. You can do experiments purely for your own amusement, earn frankly stupid amounts of money, have exciting adventures, engage in decades-long battles of wits with worthy adversaries, and not even have to turn up to a specific place to work each day.

For so many people, the main reason their work life sucks so much is because they've never had a great job. And the best way to get a great job is to create one yourself. Reporting to you, rather than letting others set the terms. As an employee, no matter how much you earn, no matter what sort of exalted 'Vice-President' you are, you're still someone else's bitch for all your working days.

It's the endless uncertainty that gets you when you're dancing to someone else's tune. Particularly if your industry, like mine, has been run over by a convoy of buses in recent times. What if there's no return to the warm embrace of work like it used to be?

At night, you wonder if all your hard-won skills and experience will end with you on a bicycle, thighs burning uphill in the dark, a venture capitalist's dinner on your back. When you drift at the mercy of external forces for months, potentially years, with no sense of control, powerlessness can set like a plaster cast. You worry that future office skills will be based on some *Fortnite*-style platform pitting surviving workers against each other in a mortal productivity battle, and the victors will be heads-down nineteen-year-olds who can't even string a sentence together.

Where you go from here depends on your ability to see change as your friend. Change isn't an easy friend to live with. But if you can put up with its tantrums and mood swings, change will help you cut a path through the crowd. You can get to places most others will never reach. Most people would rather suffer and complain than face change. That's fine, because it means you and I can reap the benefits.

The true greatness of business is that it's a long game. Models, pop singers and sports stars enjoy the good times early, peak at thirty, and it's all downhill from there. By age fifty, it's 'Do you know who I used to be?' Every so often you see one of the sports stars of your youth, brutally aged by all that sun exposure, giving speeches to shiraz-soaked financiers, eternally reliving the years when they mattered. Or entertainers doused in supermarket hair dye, playing a set of their two hits at a *Remember Your Favourite Decade?* revival gig. But in business, you spend the whole time getting better and better at it, building on your mistake-infested early years, slowly becoming wilier than a coyote who's realised he can just catch road runners when they're asleep.

Screw nostalgia. Spare us your good old days. If your business is working as it should, the best time is *now*. Business gives you that tingly sensation that something interesting is around the corner. Without that sense of greater things ahead, you're on a decline that ends with you in a pub up the coast, at a poker machine with your first discount-coupon drink at 11 am.

Business lets you maintain the rage. The adrenaline buzz of being able to do *anything* once you get your cash flow working. Sure, it's not for everyone. Plenty of people enjoy being safe in a box so they don't have to face their personal nightmare of dealing with infinite free-form possibilities. Like those videos of animals released after years of brutal captivity, who take a hesitant look at the lush green world outside before turning back to their cage. They feel calm and secure in there, with its blissful freedom from decisions.

But once you get the hang of freedom, it's intoxicating. You can do whatever the hell you like without having to justify it to management, shareholders, analysts or anyone else with an opinion they'd like to throw in.

If you start a business, you are performing a very slow magic trick: creating something out of thin air. It's not like having a job where you take something that already exists, mess with it for a while, then pass it on to the next anonymous custodian. Your own business is a lasting monument to your own evil skills and persistence.

What could be more fun than trying to persuade high-calibre staff to defect in secret meetings in the back of darkened restaurants? All the pantomime tension ('Did anyone see you come in?') without any of the legitimate danger police or spies have to deal with. Building rela- tionships with clients you've genuinely come to regard as friends, and feeling a surge of parent-style pride when they tell you how great it is to work with your people.

Business is an endless stream of multifaceted amusement, along with the odd burst of searing pain. The pain is part of the fun. Most impor- tantly, when you get into your forties, it's the only way you can keep your pride. I see people who were bright young executives alongside me and had great careers, yet they now find themselves servants to people a decade or more younger. It's a deeply unattractive prospect and one you should work to avoid, right fucking now. It leads to scenes like forty- seven-year-old job candidates pretending they're down with TikTok, because they read it's the future of marketing. Please, have some dignity, you're creeping the kids out.

Take charge of your life on your own terms. Or your boss will do it for you one Friday when you had something else planned.

Grab a stapler and hole punch on the way out. You'll be needing those.

DETECTIVES ON
OUR TRAIL

We knew starting a business was worth it when we spotted the private investigator tailing us in a blue Ford. With our local business partner at the wheel, we took a back route to our newly leased warehouse. The PI stuck to us like a pro, but it was much slower and duller than in the movies. No handbrake turns onto freeway exits. No street fruit carts knocked over. He pulled up a discreet distance from our office and watched us perform suspicious acts: unloading new laptops from cars, setting up shelves and similar criminal mastermind activity. Disappointingly, he didn't have a newspaper with cut-out eye holes. Still, it gave our plucky little venture an outlaw image that got people talking. Cheers, giant competitor!

The idea had been brewing for a decade. It started when I was sent to a tech conference at the giant, soulless Anaheim Hilton, the most un-magical land in the Disney district. Company travel policy was twin-share accommodation. My roommate was someone called Peter, our new management recruit from a giant luxury hotel group. We had never met, and neither of us was excited by the prospect. He was not keen to spend a week locked up with a technician-turned-manager, who, he thought, would have a mullet and want to talk routers and bandwidth. Likewise, I was not amped about being cellmate with a fussy ex-hotel guy who, I assumed, would fold the toilet roll into a perfect point, order fruit platters and complain about the sheet thread count.

We met up in the lobby bar over a couple of weak American beers, found our fears were groundless, and realised we would be friends for life. A week of night-mayhem ensued. Americans are incredibly generous about having their parties invaded by Australians, and it would have been rude not to accept their hospitality. On our return, after auditing of our hotel bills, we got a permanent ban on doing business trips together. In the back of our minds for the next decade was the goal that one glorious day, we would be free to sign off on our own bar expenses. As inspiration goes it wouldn't make a great TED talk, but it worked for us.

The company we both worked for at the time was the dominant gorilla in its field, a national audiovisual company. We provided the technical side of corporate events: the epic video, sound and lighting systems that made stage stars of bank CEOs and billionaire software nerds. Our people lurked up the back of the room in the dark, pushing buttons. It's not an industry most people have heard of. To this day, I'm not even sure my own mother understands exactly what our industry does.

We had loyal, dedicated staff and a great reputation. Despite growing from a garage-sized outfit up to 750 staff, it still had a really nice communal feel. But we didn't own any of it. In the endless planes and hotels of our corporate road life, Peter and I workshopped the idea of our own venture. One day, there would be an opportunity for a smaller, boutique alternative. That's the natural Darwinian order of things. We filed it in the 'get around to it one day' basket.

The madness started a few years later when the private equity guys arrived. The original owners had been there fifteen years and wanted to cash out. In came the external investors and their cold-eyed henchmen. I was on the board, but not a shareholder – an unpleasant combo – so I saw the early signs of what lay ahead: a total lack of understanding that our staff did something specialist and difficult because they loved it. To the new overlords, it was no different to making pizzas. So I left to set up my own marketing agency. Peter stayed and watched all kinds of financier-driven madness over five years. Good people thrown into the volcano to appease the shareholder gods; expensive consultants running amok, vacuuming up all the margins. The end times were at hand. I called Peter in his hotel bunker and said, 'It's time.' We started scraping around for money to borrow.

A few weeks later, they sacked Peter and put him on twelve months' gardening leave, meaning he couldn't work for a competitor. We sketched out the plan: a national-but-smaller version of our old employer. We named it Scene Change.

It's a strange feeling to have a fully formed plan you're dying to smash into, then just park it for an entire year. When the legal all-clear blew, we decided to start the business on an island. They're easier to conquer and defend. And the private investigators are easier to spot. We flew to Hobart and asked the staff of the old outfit to join our revolution. Tasmanians tend to come as a gang, so it was one in, all in. Appropriately, we took them all to a pirate-themed restaurant in the Hobart docks. We pitched the business vision. Any questions?

'What colour's the logo?'

They were hardcore technical types. You'd think they'd ask what leading-edge technology we would buy. And what the pay was. But . . . the logo? To understand, you need some context. A year previous, the competitor's new marketing director had felt a rebrand would fix everything. They hired a design agency to create a new logo with real showbiz impact. The brief asked for something that would make people go: 'Wow!' In a scene worthy of *The Office*, the new logo was the name of the business with a lime-green cartoon talk bubble saying . . . 'WOW!'

The new look was launched to a bemused workforce. Hard-arsed, black-clad technical types got new white shirts with a lime-green *WOW!* Their vans were repainted white with a colossal lime-green *WOW!* They felt like small kids whose mothers had combed their hair down, cleaned around their mouths with a handkerchief, and made them wear long socks to a family gathering.

We hoped Scene Change might be the antidote. I had a full brand design folio ready.

'It's black. We'll have black uniforms. The business cards will be black. The vans will be black, with the darkest legal window tint. We want you to pull up to venues and look badass.'

They pored over the van designs, which read *Audiovisual Response Unit*. Each van would have its own racing number. They seemed to like the logo. Any other questions? They only had one.

'Can the vans have chrome rims?'

'Sure.'

They all looked at each other around the table, exchanging micro-nods.

'Okay. We're in.'

Appealing to customers is fine, but if your brand embarrasses your staff, all the marketing in the world won't do a damn thing. Sometimes black vans with chrome rims are all it takes.

Within ten years, the business was providing us with a seven-figure income each from profit, every year, without us needing to work there day to day. I hesitate to drop this vulgar cash chat here, but we got there by doing the opposite of many of the accepted business rules. It's important you know that it works.

WHY NOW?
ROACH SKILLS RULE

Chaos is an excellent catalyst for starting a new business. Competitors who would normally crush you are dazed and confused after COVID-19 reshuffled their deck. Their precious systems and processes are interrupted. They hate change. They're slow to move, so they're vulnerable. In *you* go, like the proverbial roach after the Apocalypse, antennae wiggling as you sense sweet opportunity. What's in that open fridge?

There's a lot to work with. So much has changed in your customers' lives. Some of them have more money; most will have less. They're rethinking their buying habits. Now is the time they'll start spending their money somewhere new.

I learnt this in frustrating fashion. We launched our business in 2006, after a bunch of potential clients said, 'Our existing supplier sucks. They're unresponsive and expensive. If only there was someone else we trusted who could offer good service, we'd change right away.'

We were up for that sweet prospect. We borrowed all the money we could and opened in four cities in year one. Looking back, I think: were we drunk? We put in proposals to all those clients. Every one came back with: 'Thanks for all your effort, but on this occasion, we decided . . . better the devil you know.' Were they calling us a devil they didn't know? Harsh, but that's the reality of being a new supplier, even if you have proven skills and they know you personally. So we knuckled down for a couple of years of self-financed cash burn. Sometimes you have to live off two-minute noodles for a while.

Then in 2008 Lehman Brothers went down, the world plunged into financial crisis, corporate budgets got slashed, and . . . the enquiries started. 'Hi, cheaper, friendlier alternative people, can you give us a quote?' It was customer habit-breaking time. We were off, and we've never looked back.

So many successful businesses set up during the hard times. Uber and Airbnb started in the last financial crisis. There are lots of advantages that will help you survive. Your costs will be down for all kinds of reasons: commercial rents are on a downward spiral that might never recover, good staff are more affordable now, interest rates are absurdly low. And most importantly, you can start with a clean, streamlined structure that suits the times. You're not weighed down by cumbersome yesteryear tech or office fitouts. Geography is no restraint for staff – it's never been easier to make your business look big, even when it's you, a laptop and your dog. There are more ways to fund a business than ever before.

It's much more fun to be the up-and-comer. We started that way, we still are, and I hope we never become the big guys. Being smaller creates energy – you have to fight for every gain, every day. Starting in hard times gives you an appreciation of new customers that never wears off. Every victory is glorious. And you have infinite options and the freedom to adapt quickly when others can't.

Big companies have a defensive mindset. They have to win huge volumes of work, every year. But when they do, there are fewer fist pumps. Mainly just relief. Because those wins are what's expected of them. It's already in their budget. They'd better make absolutely sure they win, or heads will roll. Established companies have a certain swagger, but they also spend a lot of time worrying what those upstart competitors are up to.

In situations like COVID-19, big companies say, 'We must be agile to survive these unprecedented times!' They have brainstorming meetings.

The ideas are collated for the Innovation Firestorm Committee to fast-track. Five meetings later, the best of those ideas are circulated to all department heads. After a time – these are busy people – responses are tabled on the difficulties of implementing those ideas. There are new suggestions that are more finance-, operations- or marketing-centric, from the finance, operations and marketing people respectively. A few ideas survive, which are passed on to the CFO for detailed ROI analysis, then final board presentations are prepared for approval (*checks calendar, it is now three years later*).

In that time your small company has become a successful business doing that thing that was obvious from the start. Being the upstart can be way more profitable, because you're not carrying platoons of middle-management Dereks and Brendas. The last time our industry's biggest player published their figures, we noticed that we made more profit. Not a higher *percentage* profit. We made more actual dollars than they did. Even though they were four times our size. Economies of scale can be a myth.

With the upstart mindset, the good times start from day one. Outsiders who don't get it imagine you're suffering towards a distant goal, at which point you'll go, 'Whew, I made it. Life is good. Now I can relax and drink champagne.' But the hungry early years are just as great. Sure, money is tight, but you can see your sweet future. It's clear in your mind, because that's the only way it's going to come true. So in some ways, you feel like you're there already.

You could put that decision off until one day. You might have perfectly good reasons for that: family, finance and so on. That's fine, but the odds will be tougher if you do it in five years. The good opportunities will be heavily picked over. Others will have bought at the sale and you'll be paying full price.

BUT WHAT ABOUT
THE RISK?

If you mention you're thinking about setting up your own business, here's what happens next. Your partner, friends, parents and the convenience store guy all say: 'Easy, tiger, you've got a good job. Leaving it would be pretty risky.' People fear the unknown. They love to warn you not to do things.

Enough of their 1980s salaryman thinking. Today, having a job is a huge risk. A job is like owning a business with one client. Nobody would buy that business because it would be an unacceptable risk: lose that one client and you don't have a business. Even if you don't lose the client, their hold over you is pretty dominant, and you have the negotiating power of plankton.

If you have a job and you seriously displease *one* person – your boss, your major client – you don't have a job anymore. That decision is entirely out of your control. They can decide to get rid of you at any moment, regardless of your performance.

Maybe you've done a terrific job but they decide to get rid of 20 per cent of the workforce to cut costs. You can probably get another job, but perhaps you can't. I know people in lucrative gigs who fear they're in their last job. Because employers will swap them for someone younger and cheaper, leaving them with a world of ongoing expenses they can't cover. The higher up the job ladder, the more your lifestyle expands to spend the lot. Plus your high salary makes you a tasty cost-cutting target.

A friend at a major bank put it best: 'Your direct boss cares. Anybody two levels above you doesn't know you exist.' You're just head count to them. Look at your boss's boss. Ask yourself: if their bonus depended on them firing you on Christmas Eve, would they do it? If your answer isn't a resounding 'No!' – if you had to think about it even for a moment – you know they'd do it in a heartbeat.

Another friend in finance got a new US-based global CEO, whose first act was to shut down the entire Australian operation, describing it off the record as 'a goddamn popcorn stand'. Which is a great line, but no fun if you're on the receiving end.

Jobs have always come with these risks, but never more than now, as once-dependable careers get devoured by apps, AI and low-paid Belarusian freelancers. Big business is highly aroused by the idea of making everyone a casual labourer, an excellent way to bring down fixed costs and employee entitlements. It's a digital version of the Depression-era docks, where able-bodied men would line up at dawn hoping to be the one in ten picked for a day's harsh work. Now it just gets dressed up in chirpier language. 'It's great, everyone's an entrepreneur! Work your own hours! Flexibility!' say the disruption boosters, spruiking apps that bid out menial tasks to the cheapest, most desperate individual.

This could be your future at age fifty-five: bidding to be the cheapest hamster cage-cleaner or underpants-folder for some entitled tech couple in their thirties. Be under no illusions: that is not having your own business. It's all the bad bits of having a job minus the perks and safety nets. You are not an entrepreneur. You're a seagull competing for chips.

Have a job, and you have to think twice before expressing yourself or taking any sort of risk. You waste time considering if your boss is okay with how you interpret 'business casual'. You worry about ignoring evening emails because you live in fear of being outworked by rivals. So you live out your days as an increasingly timid, downtrodden creature. What kind of insane risk is that?

Owning a business is, obviously, also risky. But as your business gets bigger you get more clients. Maybe one of them – inevitably – 'fires' you, by choosing a competitor or by not spending any money that year. That's okay, because you have five other clients. Then fifteen. The risk of one random decision taking down your whole livelihood tapers off. Particularly if you end up owning a range of different businesses, so if some nightmare event takes out one of them, it isn't everything.

So, long term, you don't have to say yes to The Man (or The Woman) all the time. The great thing is that as your risk decreases, you become less timid. Your confidence comes across to clients, leading to more new business and a general sense you're going places. You're free to walk away from rubbish clients and time-wasters. You might choose to hike up their price, so either they walk or you make windfall profits. And you're cool with either option. There is no drug that matches this feeling. Few people in a job have this luxury.

Oh, and if you have a job, do you have the chance to sell that job to someone else for a multiple of your annual earnings, like business owners can? When jobs end, you just pack up your desk, go home and start updating your LinkedIn profile, trawling for people to endorse you for 'Value-Add Skills' and wondering if you should add 'ninja' to your title.

Keep your job and be forever ruled by the random decisions of a handful of people you have no control over, who may not have your interests at heart. Is that the kind of risk your nearest and dearest would prefer you to take? Or are they willing to support you as work your way to exhilarating freedom?

2.

BUSTING THE BIG BUSINESS MYTHS

A CAR-CRASH
CAREER PATH

Occasionally throughout your life, you'll string together a consistent run of stupidity and poor choices, then think: wow, I sure wasted that time.

Chill out about that. As long as you were doing *something*, it will come back randomly to help you decades later in ways you can never predict. None of it is wasted.

Career guidance was primitive at my school. Its list of degree-needing careers spanned nine gigs: teacher, engineer, scientist, accountant, lawyer, vet, dentist, doctor and, mysteriously, forestry. They advised me: 'You will get a good mark in the final exams, so you're letting your parents down unless you do a degree with a high entry mark. Vet, dentist or doctor.'

I was a keen reptile collector as a kid. Medicine and dentistry seemed a world of grown-up responsibility, so vet it was. The idea that you could get a job in business never came up. So I left home for vet school. I learnt there are three sorts of vet students: suburban dog and cat people; rugged farm types who regard animals with the same detached cost–benefit perspective that business people apply to desk chairs; and girls who love horses.

I was fine with the dogs and cats. But farm animals were a shock. I'd never really seen them up close, as I'd been educated by picture books.

19

I thought a pig was the size of a large dog. Ordered to vaccinate one, I loaded up my syringe, jumped the fence and came face to face with boar reality. Holy shit, it was the size and shape of a Kia Carnival. It had big sharky teeth. Its tiny eyes bored holes through me, its muscles tensed to pin me to the wall and feast upon my broken carcass, like the street pigs of medieval times.

I feinted to the left, closed my eyes, and jabbed the needle home. The noise, my God. Like a thousand electric drills boring into plate steel. The sound of shrieking pigs still comes for me in my nightmares. There was more to come. We had to tattoo the pig with the farm's serial number. Parlour inking technique doesn't work on a giant, cranky porker. So they make the whole tattoo out of individual needles, affixed to a handle. Think of a giant hairbrush with nails instead of bristles. You dip the whole thing into the ink, chase down your pig, and smack it as hard as you can. Could you do that to a hipster? I'd watch that TV show.

What's that? Oh, you'd like to know how it feels to put your whole arm up a cow. It's not so bad. I did it at dawn in a savage winter, and thought: at least one arm is nice and warm. I asked the farm guys if they could back up another cow so I could defrost the other arm. They looked at me with expressions that said: get back to the city and find another career, fool.

It got worse. We had to spend two weeks on the vet school's horse farm. Horses are enormous and can kill you. We fancy-dressed in boots and checked shirts, trying to fool the locals. Day one: time to learn where horse babies come from. We turned up to the artificial insemination collection yard. A lady horse was tied up in an open-ended pen, putting out keen signals at a Lynx ad level of subtlety. The farm guys led in a colossal stallion, snorting and twitching. Two of us students were on collection duty. I got a pair of rubber gloves. My comrade got a metal flask, like part of a picnic setting. Our supervisor looked us up and down with a general air of disgust.

'Get in the pen.'

A row of locals perched on the railings, grinning, smoking and waiting for the show to start. The stallion got a whiff of the mare and became very visibly In The Mood. He stomped about and surged forward, dragging the handlers with him, then reared up, forelegs on the mare. We edged towards this thrashing stack of beasts. My task was to interrupt the stallion just before the train went into the tunnel and divert it into the flask. What would current workplace safety experts make of this?

'Your job today is to interrupt a combined two tonnes of urgent, violent horse sex with a cold metal flask.'

'Okay, do I get a helmet?'

'No, this is the '80s. Get to work, boy.'

You know when you turn on a garden hose to full pressure and it flails around uncontrollably? Think of that, but firehose size. This was what I had to get to grips with, above my head, then plunge it into the container. Against the odds, we did it. The stallion wandered off to have the horse version of a cigarette and a nap. The mare had a resigned 'Is that it?' look. The locals were disappointed at the lack of hoofprints on our teenage bodies.

What kind of nightmare had I signed up for? I whiled away the next couple of years playing horrifying jokes with animal parts on friends. I went to lectures in pyjamas. I was an out-of-control, show-off dickhead and a liability to the profession. In the exams, microscope slides of blotchy colours swam before my eyes. Important parts of animals all looked like similar cheap cuts of supermarket beef. This did not go unnoticed by the faculty.

'You are an absolute clown,' said the dean, or words to that effect. Correctly. 'You should take a couple of years off and reconsider your commitment to veterinary science.'

That consideration lasted, oh, the rest of the morning. I moved into a filthy share house with my new girlfriend. I got a cab driver's licence. Five weeks into that, I picked up a suit guy in the city. In the ten-minute ride to his office we had the usual cabbie chat. He said I seemed like a bright young fellow. Did I want a technical job in the corporate audio-visual industry? He didn't seem like a sex predator, so I said: 'Sure.' I had no idea what this job was, but it had to be better than cabs. To this day I've never done a job interview, which is just as well.

I've since grown to like pigs, too. Such a sweet animal.

YOU DON'T ALWAYS
NEED DIRECTION

So I became a corporate roadie. I learnt by being thrown in the deep end, totally unqualified, and getting yelled at. We loaded trucks full of video projectors, lighting, sound systems and stage sets into luxury hotels at dawn. The five-star experience was reserved for the guest areas. The loading docks were all puddles of fermenting meat juice from carcasses delivered straight onto the concrete, dumpsters pumping out chemical warfare levels of food scrap methane, and trolleys of rumpled linen infused with the DNA of a thousand lonely business people.

With heavy, expensive equipment in one hand and the other on a swaying twenty-foot ladder, and in direct violation of safety laws yet to be written, we turned a ballroom into a glittering theatre for an estate agent awards night, prestige car launch or pharmaceutical conference. Unfed all day, we'd watch from the back like Dickens-era orphans as corporate high-flyers feasted on salmon pinwheels, veal cordon bleu, and the prawns that 1990s hotels liked to present on metre-high ice carvings. All the guests were hammered on oaked chardonnay and Crown Lager. From our sober, button-pushing vantage point, we saw a lot of discreet wedding ring removal as the dance floor filled up. It was an open-range zoo of loose human behaviour. At midnight after the last drunks were evicted, we'd pack everything down and take it back to the factory. In busy season, eighteen-hour days were the norm.

We used the same equipment as rock-and-roll roadies, but corporate work is more stressful. Every night is opening night, with chaos and errors from presenters too busy to rehearse. People are terrified of getting up on stage, so they're mean and snappy backstage and can't think straight. When your job at age twenty-one involves calming down freaked-out CEOs backstage as they prepare to front a hostile crowd, all other meetings for the rest of your life hold no particular fear.

It was viciously demanding work and terrible for my personal life. I was a dream partner, in the sense that I was only present while my partner slept, leaving only a vague hotel loading dock aroma. As the business grew, I started doing events across South-East Asia so I could be away for weeks.

There was a boom in incentive events, which took the top-achieving insurance, computer or pharma sales execs to opulent hotels in exotic destinations and treated them like spoilt royalty for three or four days. Out of the country, their inner colonialist instincts were set free. They assumed other poorer countries had no laws applying to white sales high-flyers. How wrong they were. As it turned out, even airlines and hotels had detention powers. There would be one or two delegates who were so well-refreshed on the flight out of Australia that they were handcuffed to their plane seats. Or imprisoned for a day or so in special rooms the hotels used to dry out western drunks until they stopped insulting staff and breaking things.

I travelled so much I needed a new passport every couple of years, not because it expired but because the old one had no more room for stamps. It was intense work. Friends always said the same thing: 'Off travelling again? Can I carry your bags for you?' The reality was: fly to a plush hotel, set up the event in a dark ballroom, run the show all day, reset and rehearse most of the night, get three or four hours sleep, rinse and repeat for a week. Live off room service burgers and club sandwiches. Walk outside the hotel for the first time when you leave for the airport on the way home, blinking like a vampire in the daylight.

I watched the same corporate motivators again and again, backed by classic motivational soundtracks. *Eye of the Tiger, Simply the Best, Down Under, Tubthumping* – all tunes that made me yearn for the blessed silence of the grave. Years of megadose exposure to keynote speakers left me immune to their schtick. Many of them started with good ideas grounded in real business, but then keynoting became their business and they lost touch with reality.

Like the king of body language, who would do an hour of hot tips on the psychology of why people rub their eyes or fold their arms, with zero consideration that they might just have tired eyes or arms. His favourite theory was that in a handshake, the most powerful person would approach with the palm tilted down, asserting dominance over the weaker, palm-up person. I always enjoyed watching the menfolk shaking hands afterwards, each doing hyper-masculine contortions to avoid being the submissive one.

You can tell people pretty much all they need to succeed in about five minutes. Their challenge is finding the discipline to do it. I've summarised it for you at the end of the book, so feel free to skip through all the other tales. But people want to believe success is more complex than it is, so it gets padded out with showbiz routines and embarrassing interactions with those around you. Like half an hour into the speech when you hear these dreaded words:

'Feels like the room's a little low on energy right now. Let's get some music on! Make some *noooiiiiiise*! Now I want you all to stand up, turn to the right, and massage the shoulders of the person next to you. YEAAAAAH! How good does that feel? Keep it up! Can you feel the energy? Now, turn around and massage the person to your left!'

Please. I did not give up half my day to touch the shoulders of some random sales rep, and I especially don't want to turn around and feel his creepy sausage fingers on me. That is the opposite of relaxation. An ability to think and absorb information while quietly sitting still is a basic adult skill. Why do you think they teach it at school? If people could negotiate treaties to end world wars from a seated position, you can learn about business without getting pawed at by strangers.

You can only absorb so much of that kind of madness. After five years of sleep deprivation and the complete destruction of my social life, I had to get out. The turning point came one morning on the way to a gig. I'd set up the equipment the night before in a venue about ten minutes' drive from my house. I woke early and dressed in my technician's outfit.

Backstory: the managers of the business were obsessed with looking corporate. So rather than the black polo shirts worn by every other audio-visual technician in the world, they made us wear black business shoes, polyester slacks, a white polyester business shirt, and a black polyester tie. Embroidered logos everywhere, and all of it felt highly flammable. We complained this wasn't great for loading tonnes of road cases through hot, filthy loading docks. So they gave us black overalls with white racing stripes, with our name embroidered above the logo. To be worn *over* our sweaty polyester-wear during set-ups, and removed as the client arrived, like James Bond with the tuxedo under his wetsuit. Or we would have done, had we not put the overalls straight in the dumpster.

The morning of that final show, I jumped in my company van, which wouldn't start. Fuck! The audience would arrive soon. Idea! I banged on the neighbour's door and borrowed his bicycle. I pedalled off, down a major commuter road at peak hour, slacks tucked into my business socks, tie fluttering in the breeze. I heard yelling and a revving engine, then the whistle of an apple thrown from a vehicle at high speed, rocketing millimetres past my nose.

'Fuck off, ya fucken Mormon dickhead!' someone shouted from the passenger window.

Enough.

I took a desk job managing our technical team, and secretly enrolled in a part-time business degree at night. I had to escape this terrible industry. Our reception area was full of ad trade magazines. The alluring recruitment section offered crazy sums to people who could write ads. I could write ads, I just needed a foot in the door, and a business qualification would cover up my shameful technical- and vet-failure history. I would become a famous creative director!

I never got into an agency. My employers foiled my escape plans by making me their marketing manager and paying for my degree. They

25

sent me to America to learn from other, bigger businesses. I cursed them for their kindness in supporting whatever I wanted to do as long as it was with them. I cursed myself for saying yes to the path of least resistance. I had surrendered to middle-management comfort. My half-arsed plans and dreams started slipping away.

I'll leave out the restaurant dishwasher, the line cook, and the funfair carnie jobs – we haven't the space. But none of these career backroad trips are wasted, not a moment. I feel sorry for people who go straight from school to university to some predetermined lifetime career like dentistry or law. It seems such a stifled experience. No interesting tales to tell, not much mixing with anyone outside your tight little socio-economic cluster. No sense of pulling yourself out of the deep holes you've blundered into.

It's important to have goals, but if you do enough random activity, stuff that's not on your list just finds you. Sometimes your failures become massive long-term wins. Five years into my marketing manager gig, my burning goal was to be a witty newspaper columnist like my teenage hero, Clive James. I cut my job back to three days a week to focus on writing what I hoped to be wry observations about everyday life. My writing wasn't very good and my submissions to editors got nowhere. No Clivedom for me.

Then the business sold, the new overlords came in, and my only escape route was to set up my own marketing agency. At last, I could become a creative director, by appointing myself to that position. Congratulations, me! It was unbelievable fun for a decade. During which I realised there's an age when you have to stop being a creative director and become an adult business person. Scene Change became my escape plan and it worked.

For the last decade I've written columns for industry magazines and business websites. Unpaid, but it has a value for our business. I've seen the firestorm of redundancies that have engulfed media in recent years, and I know if I'd achieved all my dreams back then, I'd be one of a thousand unemployed column writers with no business skills. Now I've got enough money, had enough writing practice, and have the spare time to write a book for a publisher I've always loved.

Every one of the missteps, the poor choices, the pig tattooing, the stress and sleep deprivation that made me ache to be doing something else was an essential piece of the puzzle that got me to this point of existing in my own personal amusement park. I just didn't know it at the time.

Scene Change got started by providing a brand that wasn't embarrassing to our technicians, because I'd experienced the horror of those monogrammed overalls firsthand and felt the shame these terrible management ideas can cause to your staff. Without that, I would have been just another marketing creep saying: 'They can wear what we tell them. That's why we're management.'

You just have to approach everything like you *do* own the company. Eventually, the constant diversions and apparent dead ends pay off, and you're trained and ready to run your own place. Thank God. I could have been looking at an entire life of fisting cows or dental-flossing French Bulldogs. The thought makes me feel ill.

BLOCKED BY THE THREE BIG BUSINESS MYTHS

So many smart, skilled people are worried they can't take the entrepreneur plunge, because all their lives they've been fed the Three Big Myths About Business:

1. You need to be a numbers wizard.
2. You need relentless hustle.
3. It's all about ordering people around and general dick-swinging like in *The Apprentice*.

It's a shame, because those barriers are imaginary, or relics of a bygone time. You can still do those things if you want, but you can do fine without them.

Let's bust Myth One. Can you add up and do percentages on a spreadsheet? That's all you need. We'll go into more detail later, but the art of management is knowing which numbers really matter. Your business will live or die by a handful of ratios. For us, there's just three. If you obsess over every measurement, your business will feel like hectares of spot fires and you'll drive your staff mad.

At business school, you learn to build clever spreadsheets to assess investment projects. You calculate the net present value of future cash flows against the up-front outlay, and the spreadsheet spits out a neat yes or no answer. It's a good brain exercise, and essential if you're building a toll road or power station. You aren't. If you need to do that sort of analysis for your own project, dump the project. You're applying science-y method to future numbers that are guesswork jacked up with optimism.

When my partners and I discuss investments, if they can't be justified on the back of a coaster, it's not profitable enough to proceed. If you passed primary school maths, that'll do for business.

Myth Two: the hustle. It can be super annoying. Hustle makes you talk about yourself all day, in person and in LinkedIn videos shot in your car: 'Yo, wassup! Gonna give you the lowdown on sales funnels!' Hustle makes you harass customers with promo emails and texts every day. Meanwhile, professional selling has evolved towards low-hustle skills: listening, learning, empathy and understanding customers' lives, leaving the hustle bros looking like extras in *The Wolf of Wall Street*. Persistence and endurance are vital, but you don't need to be pestering everyone 24/7.

Which leaves us with Myth Three: *The Apprentice*-style shows of dominance. Businesses were once gorilla colonies, ruled by one dominant silverback whose orders were law. You had to jump to it or there would be punishment and humiliation. *My way or the highway. I alone know how to deliver excellence, so be more like me.* Emotion, uncertainty and admissions of fear were clear signs you weren't cut out for the rugged business life.

Things are much less primal now. People still want a strong leader, but strength has different dimensions in uncertain times. The ability to listen, guide and inspire outperforms the big stick and bigger ego. What makes people work when you're not there? Sure, you can try the sinister prison-surveillance tech that big companies love right now. Amazon has patented wristbands that log your warehouse box-picking speed and send you instant messages if you drop below the herd average. Other Amazon tech generates automatic termination notices to save the cost of having a human fire you.[1] These *Terminator* Skynet methods might be effective for keeping a desperate, churning workforce in line, but they're not going to help someone have a good idea, are they?

It's up to you to create an environment where people want to do their best work. With that in mind, what new skills are hot now? Some level of creativity is all that'll save you from robot replacement in the long run. The most valuable skills in recent times are the ones that have evolved beyond the gorilla management era. The ability to listen, sense how people feel, and get them to open up. Encouraging group work and collaboration without needing to be the centre of attention every time. Not talking over people in meetings.

Now that interference from your home life is an everyday part of work, it opens the entrepreneur door to more women with families. That's been a huge waste of brainpower until recently. Who has the skills to manage a bunch of different remote work activities at once? Who's match-fit for the randomised human chaos of business? Come on down, mums.

It was nice to see so many guys broaden their approach recently. Admitting that things aren't 'all good' is fine. People are better able to strip away the corporate mask and be the real them, honest about their fears and their weaknesses. It feels good. Turns out clients and workmates can handle it. So many colleagues have emerged as better, stronger people, and they'll enjoy life more in the long term because they can hear those inner voices more clearly.

Don't let the mythology stand in your way. I'm pretty sure I'd get fired on the first episode of *The Apprentice*, and I worked out how to build businesses. You'll cope just fine.

YOUR SUCCESS GOALS
ARE BUILT ON LIES

Everyone wants to be successful. Why wouldn't you? Yet few have a clear idea of what success is. Ask and people say: piles of money. Fridge full of Moët. 100K followers. Standard tick-a-box answers put in your head by people who don't know you.

As a spotty junior executive, I pored over the business high-flyer stories in magazines. The shining path to success was clear. Start a business! Work hard! Pitch it to investors and get funding to grow! Then the pinnacle of achievement: take it to IPO! Get a big house and car and boat and live the dream life! Stop working in your early forties, kick back and enjoy the fruits of all your labour! Job done, all boxes ticked. Happiness achieved.

Business magazine dreams turn out to be as illusory as Get Rock-Hard Abs or Drop Three Dress Sizes In A Month. Let's deal with them one by one, starting with the big one – the IPO (Initial Public Offering, where you take a company public). I didn't float a business but I spent a decade working for one that went public, and was on their board leading up to it. If you like having every freedom you hold dear being taken away by creepy overconfident finance types, then by all means float.

If you've owned your own business for more than a couple of years, you become quite unemployable, in the sense of your willingness to

31

take direction the way employed people do. You'll have enjoyed making quick, committee-free decisions in the best interests of the business. That speed and flexibility are one reason your business is a success. You don't want to be taking orders from people who know much less about the business than you. You don't want to fill out endless reports for your new overlords. You don't want to ask permission to do what you know to be right.

Float, or bring in private equity investors, and that's your life from now on. Investors and analysts are pulling your strings. You've gone from King Kong to organ-grinder's monkey in an adorable tiny fez and vest. Dance, little monkey! Shake that coin tin!

So many aspirations sound awesome when you're twenty-four and then turn out to be heavily flawed. Like the success seminar tales of people with a geared rental property portfolio that lets them retire at forty. Imagine you did that. Exactly what are you going to do for the next forty years of your life expectancy? You can only do so much golf, yoga or sitting around in cafés. And with who? Your friends are still consumed by work and wrangling kids. Nobody wants to catch up and hear your tales of endless leisure. So you end up golfing with club members twenty-five years your senior. Really, is running with the retired bank manager posse the success you pictured?

If you retire at forty, good luck to you, but it's a clear sign you've failed at finding something thrilling to do with your working life. David Bowie is a hero to me, not just because he wrote some sweet tunes, but mainly because he worked right up until the day he died. Sure, he wasn't behind the counter at a pool supplies store, but still, work is great. A major point of evolving as a human is to find the tasks that give you that tingle of achievement. Bowie checked out knowing he couldn't have packed a single extra accomplishment or fascinating experience into his life.

It's easy to forget how life-affirming it is to *matter*. When you run a business, people value your opinion. People want to have a word, talk about a deal, see what you think – all the interactions that make you feel clever and accomplished. The moment you lose that is the moment you start to die.

It may take decades, but you see people become invisible and irrelevant to those they used to draw energy from, with nothing to think about except their next meal and the next visit from the grandkids. Those are great things, but they shouldn't be your *only* things. At your funeral, will they sum up your life with: 'They made so much money early on, doing things they didn't like, that they were able to spend the last half of their life just being lazy.'

Considering what they'll say in your eulogy is an underrated method for getting your priorities in order. Try it.

SHOULD YOU START YOUR OWN BUSINESS?

The cruellest hoax of business books and motivational speakers is the fantasy that you can do anything: that it's all about correct goal setting, which you must write down and pin to your bedside lamp. And that if you activate the 90 per cent of your brain you're currently 'not using' – motivators *love* pseudoscience – you can achieve anything you set out to do.

No, you can't. Deep down, you know it to be true. I do. I am crap at so many things. I can't do any of the 'man skills': hanging things on walls, fixing broken household items, reversing trailers. Bunnings fills me with fear. I could do a handyman training course every weekend for life and I'd still struggle to assemble an IKEA hall table.

My greatest failed effort is meditation. Every story about business winners mentions their meditation habits. They all do it, many twice a day. They 'just feel so refreshed' afterwards. I so want to feel that refreshed. I want to be balanced in mind, body and spirit. Over the years, I've put thousands of hours into meditation practice. I've used soundtracks, apps, advice from psychologists. I've sat in all the positions and focused on all the breath and body parts.

Not once have I felt afterwards: *I meditated then.* It's not that I lack focus. But in my heart I know: *I was just sitting there.* I will never be deep-down refreshed. Sometimes you have to admit defeat. Everyone has different skills, and that's just fine.

My friend Michael is a natural-born, top-of-the-food-chain business predator. He's been obsessed with business since he was a tiny lad. By the time he was thirty, he owned six pharmacies. He'd bought the Ferrari that had been on his wall in motivational poster form since we studied together.

Yet somehow, in his late twenties, he became infected with the inspirational goal of becoming a professional golfer, despite having played no competitive golf before. Nothing devours time more greedily than golf. He spent every day doing the hundreds of chip shots and putts needed to embed excellence deep in his muscle fibres. He spent big on video analysis of his swing. Each day he would visualise his future self holding the US Open trophy aloft. He broke the news to his wife that it was time for a life in US motels working his way up through the minor tournaments.

The fuck was he thinking? It was like watching Usain Bolt take up Morris dancing. This motivator-borne virus erased several years of his productive life before he recognised it for the delusion it was. He refocused on his business, bought a large winery and built a concert amphitheatre on it. The Stones and Springsteen have played on his front lawn – golf could have cost him that. Stick to what you're good at.

The idea that you can start your own business needs the same shot of brutal reality. Or rather, the idea that your business will still be standing in ten years. It isn't easy, and the old truism that seven out of ten new businesses fail seems underestimated to me. Despite seeing themselves as the backbone of the nation, a great many small business owners couldn't run a choko vine over an outhouse.

I spent my high school years on the Gold Coast. The late radio genius Richard Marsland once pointed out that 'Gold Coast' is the universal adjective to add sleaze to any noun. 'Businessman' sounds respectable elsewhere. 'Gold Coast businessman' is code for 'property fraudster' or 'meth kingpin'. Would you entrust your livelihood or freedom to a Gold Coast lawyer? A Gold Coast model is an escort or bike gang girlfriend.

Yet the urge to make every day a holiday lures swarms of people to quit their corporate jobs and move to the Gold Coast. Where, like a holiday, there is virtually no work for them.

So they pursue their lifelong dream of opening a shop relating to their favourite hobby, like Ned Flanders's Leftorium in *The Simpsons*. With no retail skills. That shop space will be up for re-letting within the year, in the Arcade of Broken Dreams. Retail is a totally separate universe to the rest of business. Good retailers have been hanging around in shops since they could walk, soaking up all the tricks from their hard-working mother and father whose life was that store. They know retail like a salmon knows it's time to swim upstream to breed. They don't have to think, it's pure instinct.

Accountants and financial planners will tell you how often they stop corporate people with a redundancy package from 'buying a nice little café'. The events industry is full of people who have hosted a nice party or two and friends have told them: 'You should do this for a living.' As in many industries, the only barrier to entry is the budget to knock up a quick website and a box of business cards. Then another clueless wannabe joins the herd, an unmarked hazard for clients with a taste for a bargain quote.

You do need to like the sales side of business. *Every* interaction in your own business is sales. Obviously, there are the customers. But also staff, distributors, investors, bank managers, your neighbours who complain to the council about noise – the list is endless. If you can't persuade people, you're not going far, and you'll do it alone.

I've seen product geniuses and operational experts start businesses believing they can process their way to success using digital marketing, algorithms and no human contact. But no human involvement creates no team and no fans. You need to be comfortable speaking to people.

And don't tell me the game has changed and the new generation of clients just uses messaging. Our youngest business partner – he became an equity owner at twenty-one – spends hours on the phone. He gathers masses of interesting, valuable information, and all the essential non-verbal vibes you only get from voices. This is why he's a star of our industry, while others plod around the level playing field of emails and messaging.

Should you start your own business?

You need to be fascinated by people. What they do, why they do it, what they're thinking, and how all that relates to what they *actually do*. It's a lifelong study. Some people lock off the 'incoming information' valve at age twenty-five. Those people are only useful for data-processing work.

If you've worked for large companies all your life, it's harder setting up your own business. It's not impossible, but you have been taking a lot of support for granted. Wages, for example. If you work for big business, wages are just a utility, their regular appearance no more remarkable than water from the office kitchen tap. Set up your own place and the concept of wages becomes far more vivid. You check the bank account and there's not enough to cover payroll, which is in three days. Sweating late at night, you go through your accounts receivable. A couple of clients are a month overdue paying invoices. You call them up the next day and they promise to look into it. But because they work for larger companies and they get clockwork visits from the Wages Fairy, their sense of urgency isn't quite as bright red as yours. You call again two days later and they've forgotten again.

Finally, one of them makes a transfer the night before wages are due. You pay your staff. Maybe you don't pay yourself this time. You're conscious that with each payday, your superannuation, payroll tax, GST and other liabilities are jacking up, and will need to be sorted out in the next few months. You know that when the Grim Reaper comes a-knocking for businesses, it's almost always a Tax Office official underneath the black robes.

Wages are only the start of the support you don't enjoy when you run your own business. In a big business, it's easy to assume your own awesome self is the number one selling point for your clients. It can be quite the surprise to find that, as CEO of Your Surname Consulting Pty Ltd, those same clients won't take your call. Big brands are important for a lot of clients. There's an old saying in the ad business about the attraction of big clients to big agencies: 'Elephants fuck elephants'. Later, in 'For all your marketing needs', we'll discuss how to dress up like an elephant, but most likely those client elephants will still swipe left.

Even if you win the business, it's amazing how much taken-for-granted support big companies offer. Selling is hard. Delivering is harder, and you can't pull in any of those under-occupied desk people you once used back at Megacorp. All the stuff you once just ordered off the cuff you now actually have to pay for *before* you can get your eager hands on it. Back then, you cursed the IT department with their patronising eye rolls and talking down to women. Now, as you realise you lost a month's work because your hobby-grade backup IT system failed, you'd give anything to have them patronise you one more time.

Back then, when you were putting together a business tender, you would pop down the hall where some in-house expert had all the insurance currency certificates and other dull-but-essential filler you need. Now that's another two days of emails chasing up an insurance broker, for whom you are now just a minor annoyance.

If you've worked for smaller businesses, you know this. But for others, it can come as a terrible shock to bail out of the luxury liner and find yourself adrift in a tiny life raft on the high seas of business.

People with hard-to-please life partners should not set up their own business. I've not experienced it myself, but I've watched it at close quarters with staff and business partners. You throw away the security of 'a perfectly good job' but sell the partner on how it's going to make you more successful long term. They picture swift material success, plus you'll do *less* work because *you are the boss*. Others will be doing the heavy lifting while you're cruisin' down E-Z Street.

The amazing amount of work required may come as something of a shock to your partner. They may not understand that you do that work because you find it fun and stimulating. After a time, business travel will become a blessed respite. If that's you, keep your corporate job, avoid the inevitable home conflict and enjoy the rest of a life of eternal soul-destroying work drudgery, all the time walking on eggshells at home defending your work hours. You won't fix that situation with any pay rise.

You should not go into business if you think it will make you rich quickly. It won't happen. If you're going to do it full-time, you will need at least enough money to trade for about a year without any clients at all. You'll probably find some customers, but you might not, and if that happens, you don't want to be knocking on your old employer's door going, 'Sorry I left, do you have any jobs?' I've watched that happen to old workmates. A moment's silence for the tragic passing of their self-esteem.

3.

LET'S GET STARTED

SNIFFING OUT OPPORTUNITY IN THE RADIOACTIVE WASTELAND

In 2020, COVID-19 trashed a lifetime's set-in-cement daily habits across the world. Changes that huge present so many opportunities that can be hard to spot at the time, yet they will be so obvious in the rear-view mirror. You'll look back at the pre-change world and think: how the hell was that madness ever normal?

Until the late 1960s, women working in the public service and major banks were forced to resign as soon as they married. Because why would you employ someone who was going to have babies right away? No exceptions, until the rule was killed off by ocean daredevil Prime Minister Harold Holt.

Think of the decades of massive change in business that followed. The rise of the childcare industry. The convenient opening hours of supermarkets that once did office hours only. Houses that grew huge on double incomes. Meal delivery becoming a staple service. Entire industries that barely existed before.

Fast-forward to now. So many things that were fine at work just a couple of years ago now seem as antiquated and insane as firing newlywed women.

In 2019, any evidence of family interruption at work was regarded as frightfully unprofessional. Plenty of people faked excuses so they could go to deal with a child situation. Now kids and pets wander in and out of shot in your virtual meetings, and if they're not interrupting much, who could honestly see a problem with that?

Until February 2020, you were still okay – in fact, you had a moral duty – to come to work with obvious disease symptoms and cough and sneeze all over people. Because you didn't seem *that* sick, and there were deadlines. What were we all thinking? Open YouTube and trawl through decades of Codral's 'Soldier On' cold-and-flu pill ads. It's a superspreader horror show. Red-nosed, watery-eyed workers honking into tissues, then dosing up so they can get in among a crowd of their co-workers all day. Because 'people are depending on you'.

Remember how little handwashing went on? I can only report on the male side, and it was pretty sketchy. If people bothered going to the basin, it was mostly a quick soapless splash. Even though medical professionals have been telling us for centuries that the single best way to avoid disease is to wash your hands, you filthy animals.

Nobody knows for sure what it all means for business. The more certain anyone is on the details of what will happen, the more likely they're full of bullshit. But we're in for years of cascading change as all this new behaviour plays out. We can safely assume boom times in health care. Likewise home enhancements, as people realise they're going to spend a lot more time there. Home delivery logistics will boom. Home video studios. Renewable energy, which will win despite last-ditch government efforts to nobble it. We can assume the surge to online over physical retail will continue. These are obvious areas and big players are already sending in the troops.

Consider the remora fish strategy: they attach themselves to sharks and cruise along underneath, living on the shark's leftovers. During the gold rush, every chancer and grifter in the country descended on a few creek beds to make their fortune. Some did. Most didn't. They all had to eat, though. My ancient ancestors set up a bakery in Beechworth, in the Victorian goldfields, and by all accounts it did well. Same today: in the midst of the tech boom, I'm happy as a humble supplier to large tech events.

What can you sell to industries that are booming themselves? Companies that are growing fast are better to deal with. Their staff are stretched, so they don't take nine meetings to approve a $5000 purchase. Handled right, you can grow with them.

What exactly should your business do? People have lots of brainwaves about new businesses, inspired by their own personal interests. Or by the thoughts of a focus group with a sample size of one: their friend who holds tiny tea parties for their pug. That's why most of them fail.

There's a mythology of great eureka moments, the all-new genius idea that changed the game. There will always be a few, and they make a cool story, but the odds are not good. An idea is not a business. The dull reality of commerce is that it's 5 per cent genius new idea and 95 per cent hiring the right people, finding distributors, juggling cash flow, and all the other boring business skills that need detailed attention, or your business gets rinsed.

Here's where to start thinking: in a field where you work now. Or at least have a few years' commercial experience. Where you have evidence that people are willing to spend money. That way, you've already part-tested it with no risk to yourself. You have contacts. You know the right questions to ask when you're recruiting. Look at those existing customers and find out what makes them dissatisfied. Solve those problems. Otherwise, your new business idea is random guesswork.

We invested in a pet startup recently because it was a new solution to a legit problem. Its founder, Evan the vet, started the company after he put down sixteen animals in a single day. All would have been preventable with regular tick and worm treatment. Instead they got either no treatment, or Facebook vet remedies like garlic juice or cosmic lamplight, and it killed them.

'Fuck this,' said Evan. A phrase so often the start of a good business idea. He realised he could keep far more pets alive with large-scale preventative treatment. So he quit clinical vet practice and started Fleamail. Once a month, we send out a blue envelope with all the parasite treatment your pet needs, and you give it straight to your pet. The correct dosage is checked by a vet. It's as much a reminder service as online shopping. Anyone who owns a pet knows the feeling:

'Did you worm the dog?'

'No, I thought you did it.'

'Didn't you? I swear I saw you do it.'

'That was last month. Or was it the month before?'

The beauty of the Fleamail concept is that you get home, find the blue envelope in your letterbox, walk through the door and your reminder is right there: an excited pet jumping up and down. Everything in the envelope goes into or onto the pet, job done. They're safe for another month.

There are positive experiences built into the whole system, because Evan's a vet and he gets pets and owners. Even then, it was a punt, but it's working very nicely. If Evan had started an online store selling printer cartridges – which he actually did when he was younger, because a success seminar told him to – we wouldn't have touched it. What new idea can you try in your own field, with the paying customers you know and understand?

Avoid starting a business in so-hot-right-now fields. Don't start a fashion label. Or open a cocktail bar. Or become a fashion shoot stylist . . . unless you have godlike talent, and are willing to endure years of break-even desperation. These industries attract talent-impaired scenesters willing to work for free, which spoils it for anyone who charges for a legitimate service. The profits are to be made in dull, uncool industries where most people are there for business, not just to be seen with influencers and scrounge free drugs.

The more boring your potential field, the better. Try this test: does it make for a beautiful photo? If so, find a different product. Beauty, fitness, boutique hotels: these are all heavily fished-out territories. You never saw a hot photo of aged-care accessories. My friend's super-successful asphalt paving business has the ugliest damn Insta feed you'll ever see. Which makes it a less crowded field, and more lucrative if you can get it right.

Most people dream up products they and their friends would buy. So here's another avoid-the-crowd question: who's got money? Hmm, let me think. Which generation has had the whole financial board tilted towards them all their lives? Who got free university? Cheap houses? Tax breaks on all the investment properties they bought, secured against their original cheap home? All kindly subsidised by younger taxpayers? Oh yes, it's boomers.

On average, compared to the rest of the population, boomers are awash with cash. They've mostly finished supporting their dependants. They get endless government deals like franking credit top-ups. They're not hard to reach, either. They're all over the Boomer Channel aka Facebook. Talk to your parents, their friends and relatives. What's going on there that they need? (Tip: though they may look super-old to you, do not portray them as old in your marketing, or it's game over.) They have spare cash, because they missed at least two years of being able to go on Rhine River cruises hosted by a nineties TV personality. A minimum twenty grand spare right there, unless they bought a motorhome.

Yes, many older folk have embarrassing tech skills. Don't roll your eyes at them, it's a huge opportunity. Come up with ways to make tech products and services easier to use. There are literally millions of older people who find online shopping and other digital experiences a confusing nightmare – hi, Mum! – and would pay for a way to make this experience friendlier. It's a whole untapped market, an alternative to a million startups whose founders target their own tribe.

Another direction to break free from the tech herd: what's the first word that springs to mind when you think of big tech companies? Yep, 'evil'. They deliver evil in so many democracy-undermining ways, but also right up there is their delight in making non-salaried people work for below-poverty wages. Take Spotify, a company renowned for paying musicians slap-in-the-face royalties while its CEO counts his current $5 billion wealth. Artists can make more from selling 400 vinyl records than 2 million stream plays. Non-platinum musicians fucking hate Spotify, and justifiably so.

But music customers *like* musicians. Bandcamp is getting a lot of traction because it pays musicians fairly. You can choose what you pay artists. When COVID-19 hit and gigs stopped, music fans realised their favourite artists were struggling. More than 40 per cent of Bandcamp buyers paid more than asking price at checkout. Good businesses attract good customers – 'good' in the full, moral sense of the word. Bandcamp is nowhere near Spotify size, but it's growing fast.

I think there's going to be a backlash as the average consumer realises how much big tech pockets at the expense of their 'contractors', while paying no tax. We're picking up their tab. Delivery riders are getting injured and killed riding on roads that big tech doesn't help pay for. In a few decades, we'll have a generation of workers with no retirement savings because big tech skirted that obligation. While local businesses pay full-whack tax and comply with the safety laws big tech avoids.

Some people will pay more for alternatives that do the right thing. Can you take a brand that's straight-up evil and devise an ethical version? You may say, 'Being worth $5 billion for screwing poor people seems pretty cool – I'll take my chances on the bad karma,' but there can only be one or two of those in any category, and the chances of becoming one are microscopic. The odds of becoming a smaller, but viable, niche operator are so much higher.

Should you buy into a franchise? No. NO! Most of them are the closest thing to legal slavery. You do the work, others get the benefit.

Then you have to work out what your business will actually *do*. You can sell items, sell labour, a combination of the two, or, like us, rent items. Avoid making it *all* labour: it's a nightmare to make money. People often set up businesses where they mark up the hourly cost of their staff by 25 per cent and think that's a business with a 25 per cent margin. No, that is a shortcut to your inevitable date with the liquidator.

The classic pricing model for pure service businesses is to multiply the hourly cost of labour by three. A third is your cost of labour. A third is on-costs (the amount you pay on top of wages to keep people employed: phones, desks, payroll tax, insurance, toasted sandwich makers). And a third is, theoretically, profit, but the reality is much tougher. Giant professional services firms can do it. They have armies of keen up-and-comers willing to work til they drop for a sniff at the lucrative partner life some day. They work with big companies who view $600 an hour for each of the five people in a meeting as a fair rate.

Smaller clients don't feel that way: every bill for hourly services seems too much. They want to know exactly what they got for their money and they will query your bill. There are no surprise wins, only a relentless whittling down of your margins.

Each month, you'll be juggling incoming revenue against staff salaries. Salaries never stop. Incoming work does. It's incredibly stressful. If you're a services-only business, the only way to make it easier is to charge clients an ongoing retainer (where they pay an agreed fee, usually monthly) rather than for one-off projects. Then you can sleep at night with your costs covered. But ideally, you should also sell something else to supplement your services. If you're a web development company, for instance, sell an ongoing security product for an annual fee to keep the Russian extortionists out of your code. If your only revenue is staff hours, you'll be a burnt-out stress monkey all your life, and you'll look back after decades and realise all your employees have made twice as much money from the business as you.

SHARK TANKS AND LEMONADE STANDS

Entrepreneur advice can be confusing. A *Shark Tank* guy spoke in a podcast interview about our type of business, which isn't his thing. He describes it in vivid roadside terms.

> There's lots of good-sized Australian businesses here that might have twenty to a hundred staff and the owners will probably take home a million bucks between them over and above wages . . . I'm not about that. I don't mean to be offensive to anybody but I call them lemonade stands. I'm not about lemonade stands. [I'm] about global success stories.[2]

Avoiding lemonade stands because they can't scale globally is the right advice. For him. He's heaps richer than me, and friends who've dealt with him speak highly. Don't get confused, though. Lemonade stands may suck for external investors. But, as he says, a good lemonade stand can make you a million a year. Other people can run the business day to day. Would that be enough for you? It's enough for me.

His choice is right, and my choice is also right. Choice is good. It's easy to imagine the moonshot startup is the only way, because those ones get all the media coverage. The numbers are epic. Who wouldn't want to land $200 million at IPO? Rather than the slower, humbler returns of the lemonade stand.

Let's clarify the difference between an SME (small-medium enterprise) and a startup, because many people use them interchangeably.

A startup is designed either to get big fast or flame out. It has the potential to go global, or at least big nationally. Because the product is either pure software, or it uses tech to sidestep growth barriers like the cost of retail stores. There's an expectation of huge growth rates, like 10 per cent every month, early on. That growth costs heaps, and startups are rarely profitable at that early stage.

So the founder begins the endless cycle of finding external funding. This is the trade media fodder: seed funding, angel investors, A-rounds, B-rounds and so on. Look 'em up on Wikipedia if you want details; this is not that book. Each new investment round values the business at increasingly mad amounts, based on pure growth in user numbers rather than profit.

The risk for founders is getting caught up in fundraising as if that's the main game. My inbox is all 'Scootly raised $20 million', as if those founders really got that much money. No, mostly they've diluted their ownership down to homeopathic levels, so they can work themselves to death trying to make a fuck-ton of money for rich white guys.

Tattoo this onto your face like Post Malone so you see it in the mirror each morning: *your valuation ain't zip until you get the cash out*. For most founders who make it big, that means an IPO or being bought by one of the giants. Then you face restrictions on cashing out. If you float and then cash out, it spooks the markets. As do founder face tattoos, so perhaps scratch the Post Malone idea. But it really does take a long time to get money out of businesses of any size.

SMEs are more traditional businesses. Lower risk, lower growth. Ours has grown at between 20 to 30 per cent per year since we started. Even that's quite the task to manage, finance and recruit. SMEs will not become unicorns. But they're less stressful and can make you more than enough cash.

What's right for you? It's the one you like doing. The one that suits your age, how much risk you're comfortable with, and how much money you can scratch up. There's no right answer for everyone. Be realistic about that risk. New businesses all begin with an idea that seems plausible. People email me their pitch deck for something that's at idea stage, asking if I have any thoughts. Most ideas seem like they might work. But I spent a lot of years working on ad campaigns for new products. A lot of them felt like solid-gold certainties, useful solutions for real problems. They went out into the market with a decent promo budget and . . . crickets. For whatever reason, most new products just die.

It's a baby turtle scene. Thousands of brave little reptiles flapping down the beach, the fresh scent of the sea in their nostrils, full of optimism for a long salty life ahead. Then comes a swarm of predators and one in a thousand survives.

Want to bet all you own on being the luckiest turtle on the beach? It's like buying a lottery ticket and expecting to win. You can't make it in any business without a maniacal blend of luck, optimism, and sacrifice of your personal life. Imagine doing five or six years of that and ending up with nothing.

Shark Tank guy is backing many turtles, and he only needs a couple to make it to adult size. He has deep turtle knowledge, and his risks are balanced out. It's a much safer position than being the one flapping down the dunes.

People interpret the whole 'fail fast' concept as 'start a bunch of businesses based on half-arsed ideas'. This impatient, attention-deficit approach will waste years of your life. The expectation of instant blitz-growth is stupid and goes against human nature. Almost every successful business I know took off much more slowly than the founder hoped or planned. Yet it got there in the end.

The big barrier created by human nature is fear of change. Even in times like this, where change is at an all-time high, it's tricky getting customers excited about new products. *You're* excited because you put your heart and soul into that new product. Customers aren't. They want familiar and dependable. They're resistant to change, because lately everything has changed. For many, their jobs have gone from reliable wages to outsourced piecework, while houses cost a billion dollars.

Their kids who once played in the street now sit immobile for days, fused with their devices, uninterested in the dull colours, gravitational restrictions and lame weaponry of the outside world. Intimacy, physical or emotional, got replaced by parallel phone scrolling on the couch then bed. Home became work and vice versa.

You come out spruiking your new product, thinking: get excited, people, we have a game-changing new innovation to revolutionise your life!

Customers think: what, *more* fucking change? No.

When you get all excited about your new product, visualise yourself at a concert. It's your lifelong favourite band. They come on stage, kick straight into a track that was the soundtrack to your greatest party years. Woooooo, *banger*! Then three hits in:

'Here's a song from our new album, out next month!'

Think about that feeling. 'New' isn't the winner they think it is. That's the instinctive barrier you face with new products.

Our Fleamail investment was a tested risk. Like most startups, they had a product that seemed like a good idea. But they had passed the essential test: they already had about 500 paying customers. It's effectively a subscription business, which makes it more valuable. They knew what it cost to get each new client. They just needed more cash to get more customers, and some advice on how to deal with a growing business.

That's the acid test to do as early as possible: are people willing to give you money for it? It's the age-old business skill that's ignored in startup world, as if revenue is a redundant concept, like telegrams. User numbers are nice, and might help you flip the business to some company that's building another house of cards for an IPO. But unless you can get people to pay, your numbers just make you a gamer, not a business person.

The good part of startups is they allow hypergrowth, with no need for physical offices everywhere, fewer staff and so on. The bad part is that you have fewer defences against others who are doing the same. Particularly if your giant competitors decide it's easier to copy your product and bundle it with theirs, like Instagram did to Snapchat. Startups shine bright, but for many there's a short shelf life before they become a *remember when?* product. Hello Chatroulette, Second Life and

FourSquare. When grown-ass adults would publicly declare themselves the Mayor Of Their Local Supermarket. What a time.

Scene Change is loaded up with expensive capital equipment, hard-to-find staff, and painstakingly built relationships with clients. It took a decade to assemble, and if anyone else wants to play in that space, they're welcome to come on down and face the same formidable time and capital barriers. Yes, sometimes a software platform takes a savage bite out of capital investment companies, like Airbnb did with hotels. But videoconference platforms will not replace the live events we do: anyone who remembers the horror of Zoom drinks can vouch for that. The classic SME model still has plenty of life in it.

STARTUPS: A SECOND OPINION ON THE UNICORN BAIT

Some startup people will read this book and think: this guy doesn't get it, all that stuff about being nice to your staff, protecting your equity and not aiming for IPO is weak and doesn't apply to my new venture. Get out of the way, unambitious regular-economy dinosaurs, it's domination time! So I got a second opinion from people who started their business the same year we started ours.

John the photographer and I shot a lot of ads together in my agency days. He's an ex-photojournalist with an international track record. One morning in 2006, I turned up to his studio and there were three designer-types sitting around a trestle table in the loading dock, working on their new business. One was John's daughter Cyan.

Cyan and her husband Collis's freelance designer blog soon got solid international traffic. They gave me tips for my early blogging efforts. Their blog for freelancers evolved into FlashDen, a site selling modular Flash animations. Over the next decade they changed their name to Envato and became a global marketplace for creative services – design, photography, coding and music.

Now they have over 600 staff around the world, and they just celebrated a milestone of generating US$1 billion in income for their artist community. I love their story because they ignored – sometimes unconsciously – most of the startup rules.

They respect and support the creatives in their global community, in a field crowded with lowball sweatshops pitting freelancers against each other in a race to the bottom. Because when they started, they *were* online design freelancers. I've tried all those sites, and my experience has been that Envato's designers do better work. Who could have predicted that paying people a bit more might attract better people?

Envato looks after its staff in other ways. It doesn't use the regular share option scheme, because that doesn't work with a private company. So instead, Envato gives their staff a share of profit. In 2020, it was $3.75 million, 20 per cent of their annual profit. Another 2 per cent goes to charity.

They did it without external investors. It's still owned by the original four founders. They financed all that growth by creating a product that people would pay for, like normal businesses have to.

A thing I really like about Envato is that it might be a 'unicorn' business (the trade term for startups valued at over $1 billion), but Cyan and Collis just aren't interested in getting it valued. That lack of a headline number drives journalists mad. It's a relentless question in interviews. The four shareholders don't want to sell or do a capital raising. So why bother going through the hassle of paying analysts to give them that number, just to generate a headline? It doesn't mean they're less committed to the business. They're just driven by different goals.

For the first couple of years it was an evenings and weekends project, supported by doing client design work in the day. I asked if they ever saw it getting that big. That was not the original plan.

'Our ambition was to have a business on the internet,' Collis said.

'And travel,' Cyan added.

The big sites were slashing the margins they paid creatives. So they set up a site 'by designers for designers'. Cyan and Collis saved up enough money to travel overseas for eighteen months, working on Envato remotely. They hired their first developer, who brought on a developer friend, then more. Collis's brother Vahid kept an eye on things in Australia.

'He called us in Paris and said, "I think you need to come back. You kind of have an office now with five devs, and they're all working without any guidance from you."

'We came back to Australia, moved to Melbourne where the devs were, and had to learn to run a business,' said Cyan. 'We were fairly naive about it all. As it grew, things kept breaking and we needed to keep hiring people to fix it. It was years of intense problem-solving. We didn't even realise how unusual that growth was.'

They had the approaches from venture capital (VC) investors, but it wasn't their style.

'VC pushes people to get big,' said Collis. 'We still have a small mindset, we don't have to be the biggest game in town. "Go big or go home" is such a binary approach. Why not aim for moderately big?'

They were worried about losing control, and that external investors might change the values they'd created. They were free to make a lot of decisions that weren't about short-term returns. They also saw how VC affected other startups.

'Tech companies with funding can be very fast and loose with cash,' said Cyan.

They kept it super-frugal and worked like dogs. They lived in the parental basement. They drew no salaries for two years. Even when they had forty staff, they still did all the small business details themselves.

'We still took the bins out. In retrospect, we probably took the cost control too far, but we were terrified something might go wrong,' Collis said.

Their internal culture is far from the standard startup vibe Collis observes elsewhere.

'In so many companies, everyone has to have this fighting mentality, you have to be on guard to protect your interests. People like that end up in charge of businesses, so everyone assumes that's how it needs to be. We're still competitive with our competitors, but not within the business. You don't have to prioritise financial decisions over all else. We recognise that's a privileged position and we want to protect that,' he said.

Their top KPI priority isn't the sales or profit of the business itself; it's the flow of revenue to their community of sellers. It works. They make plenty of money in a game that often celebrates endless years of losses.

'Any amount of money we made even ten years ago was enough,' said Cyan. 'It just meant we have more responsibility to be sensible with it and do some useful stuff.'

For Cyan, the most fulfilling part of business was the early creative process: creating something that didn't exist before, then pulling a team together to make it reality. Getting people excited by the unlimited possibilities.

'When it gets to a certain size, it's not quite as much fun anymore,' she said.

So she unwound from Envato to start new businesses. Her current focus is Hey Tiger, a handmade chocolate brand and social enterprise. They work with The Hunger Project to help cocoa farming communities in Ghana.

Collis recently stepped back from the business and appointed a CEO who shares their values.

'It's so exciting to see someone else losing sleep when for years, that was me,' he said. 'I'm thinking wow, this is next-level business ownership. I was constantly stressed and just assumed I was a stress-out person. In the last few weeks I've realised maybe I was actually a chilled-out person in a stressful situation.'

Cyan and Collis have young kids. Most people running a business that size barely see their families. But they've been able to design their own reality, entirely on their own terms. Business can do that for you, even if it's on a much smaller scale than Envato, if you have your values and priorities clear. You don't have to take the unicorn bait.

THE WORLD DOESN'T NEED YOU OR YOUR PUNY BUSINESS

Still up for starting a new business? Good. But why? What's your mission?

I don't mean some empty corporate mission blather like 'Growing and enhancing shareholder value through the empowerment of our staff, customers and associated stakeholders' because that won't get anybody out of bed in the morning. Not you, and certainly not your staff.

Your mission – the reason your business exists, what some call positioning – has to be something that fits on a bumper sticker and uses short words. Most new businesses start as some variation on 'Yet another provider of things you can already buy'. Not good enough. The world doesn't need you and your puny business. You need a compelling reason why they should care you even exist.

Hint: don't focus on your product or service, but rather *how* you do it or *who* you do it for. Ask any business person what sets them apart. I've asked thousands of times. It's always: 'Oh, that's easy, it's our quality and our service.' As an insight, it's as useful as a social influencer in a life raft. It's the 'How are you? I'm good' of strategy.

When I was doing brands my task was to start with the viewpoint of the cold, detached punter who does not love the product. Business people find this detachment hard to grasp, such is the burning passion of their product love. You know it by how often you see this specific ad concept. Picture the boardroom creative pitch:

> Creative Director: We open on an everyday young suburban dad going about his daily routine when, suddenly, something grabs his attention. A love-struck look spreads across his face. Warm light bathes the scene, everything goes all slow-mo and romantic string music plays. Then we cut to the reverse angle. Everyone's expecting to see another person, but he's actually fallen in love with . . . your product!
>
> Client: That's gold. Thank God, finally an agency that understands how people really feel about this.

You see it in the deluded message when you unsubscribe from corporate spam: *Did you unsubscribe by accident?* They're thinking, *Surely everyone wants our twice-weekly special offers and news we're 'proud to announce'?* The only explanation that fits their world view is that you scrolled all the way to the bottom of the email, used the Hubble Space Telescope to find the word 'unsubscribe', then did another two clicks *by mistake*.

The more you talk to people who don't care about your product, the more realistic your sense of the task ahead will be. Start from the sceptic's viewpoint and you have to work a lot harder to find something that will genuinely excite people. But when you find it, you've fully justified that tingly feeling of being at the start of something big.

You need laser clarity on the benefits you bring. Most new businesses just say, 'We do everything,' so as to not miss any potential sales. So a locksmith tells people they deliver 'total corporate and domestic security solutions'. If you need a locksmith, you don't call them. Firstly, because you have no idea what they're talking about. Secondly, because there's nothing special there that says: among a choice of hundreds, this is the exact locksmith for you.

(As a child, I was obsessed with the brand-name contortions locksmiths used to get the coveted first listing in the *Yellow Pages*. I'd check each year to see if anyone had sneaked ahead of AAAAAAA Aardvark Advanced Locksmiths. A lost art killed by digital. Also, what a tragic nerd.)

My favourite positioning statement is on a plumber's truck I sometimes see at my usual surf beach. Their slogan is: 'We Turn Up.' That's a pretty modest statement. If you've never used a plumber in your life. But those three simple words strike a chord with anyone who has ever experienced the empty promises and Rastafarian sense of urgency of most tradies. Simple yet genius consumer insight.

Ask yourself: who can I be *perfect* for? What element of what I do will some people love? What is the most lucrative 20 per cent of my target market? What can I offer that shows I understand their needs better than anyone? Instead of being one of hundreds of sofa stores, be the sofa bed store, or the pet-proof sofa store, or the weekend delivery sofa store, or the home theatre sofa store. So when people stumble across you, they say: 'Thank God I found the right people.'

Ferdinand 'Ferry' Porsche, who ran that company during the time it developed the Porsche 911, said: 'I wanted to build cars that were not something to everyone, but everything to some.'[3] In 2017, they made the millionth 911 after more than fifty years of production.

Plan who will hate you. If some people think your brand is the absolute worst, it's far more likely others will love you. To them, using your product becomes a badge of pride: they are not like those losers in the hater camp. That's how the Apple Mac started. It's much more profitable than nobody caring either way.

Much of your brand is created by your staff talking to people. Your people want to feel they are the best at something. They need a burning mission, and that mission can't be what most business owners want: fat wads of cash. The cash comes as a by-product of the mission. Nobody's face ever lit up describing how they helped management meet Q3 profit expectations. Or how they became the sixth-largest company in their field, indistinguishable from numbers three to ten. But if your staff feel they are the best at something, you can create an unstoppable force.

Your mission has to be something your staff can say out loud without embarrassment and eyerolls. Imagine them discussing it at a barbecue with someone they just met. Compare them saying: 'I work for a sofa store that has the widest range and the lowest prices,' to 'We're a pet-proof sofa store, we only do sofas that pets can't damage.' The first sounds like an embarrassing late-night TV ad. The second is engaging and sets up a nice chat about cute pets.

What makes most business owners uncomfortable about being a pet-proof sofa store is the fear of missing out. What about people who don't have pets? We're cutting ourselves off from that revenue! Yes, you are, from the tight-arsed, tyre-kicker, get-four-quotes buyers who bring revenue but no margin. They don't feel strongly about your brand because they can't even remember your name.

But pet owners will bring you profitable business because you alone understand their needs. They'll recommend you to their pet-loving friends. All your sales staff need do is strike up a conversation about their lovely fluffy Blossom the Pomeranian and the product becomes almost irrelevant. It's a pure emotion purchase. For them, it's all about the dog love. For you, it's the sweet emotion of soaring profits.

Aside from the cash, do you want to look back and realise you built a business the same as all the others and made some money, or would you prefer to say: 'I blazed a trail where no one else had been before and created something great out of nothing'? Both are legitimate choices, but I know which I'd choose.

WHAT ABOUT . . . RUMPELSTILTSKIN?
NAMING YOUR BRAND

It's the first question your friends ask. What are you going to call it?

I was a professional namer. When I set up my marketing agency, there was already a plague of those in Sydney. Five in my building alone. So I set it up as a specialist brand-naming agency, of which there were none. It was a Trojan Horse move to get clients from the start so we could win their ongoing marketing work.

We spent a fun few years naming web startups, snack foods, software and dating agencies (how quaint the pre-smartphone era sounds now). Plus, in one bizarre month after 9/11, a machine that opened all your incoming business mail in case it contained anthrax spores.

'I've already thought of a great name,' said the proud entrepreneur, looking at me with wide, approval-seeking eyes. 'You're gonna love it, Ian. Ant Box.'

Ant Box. Of course. The obvious link between anthrax and ants. As a namer, you spend a lot of time nodding with pursed lips, thinking of a diplomatic response to the client's creative stylings. 'We'll certainly give that some consideration,' you say.

The naming caper was an interesting insight into the business mindset. Half the potential clients went: 'That's handy, a professional who can come up with an interesting, available name with a sound commercial strategy.' The other half would say: 'Thanks for your quote, but we decided to just get some friends together one night with a few bottles of red and come up with something cool ourselves.'

Welcome to marketing agency life. In few professional services do clients effectively say to your face: 'Not only do we believe that we, well-meaning amateurs and our random friends, can do a better job than you, a professional business writer, we also believe we can do that better job *when we are drunk*.'

Nobody has six drinks and then does their tax or pulls their own wisdom teeth. People think creatives are sensitive pixie-like souls, but we manage to absorb more casual insults, rejection and brazen requests from salaried people to work for free than the rest of the business world without punching anyone. Not that we could really damage anyone with our weak little arms.

Strangely, being a creative consultant is an excellent foundation for starting a company. The ability to listen to input from 999 people who tell you one thing and to still be able to think, 'Screw the rest of you, *I'm right*' is valuable sometimes.

You might not be right. But if you want to create a business that genuinely offers something new, sometimes you need to think that way. I hesitate to bring up Richard Branson, as the man is chronically overused in business literature. But imagine you were setting up a business called Virgin today. Particularly one that operated aircraft. There would be people lined up from here to Vladivostok to tell you your name was stupid, offensive and 'doesn't even say what you do'. But if you value conformity above anything else, owning your own business is not for you. Find a name that stands out and your business will grow into it.

How do you get started on a name? Start by getting a few bottles of red (joking, do not do that). Make a list of all the business names in your sector. This is the crowd you must stand out from. Notice how they're very similar?

This is due to the persistent myth that your name needs to say what you do.

1. Functional Names

That is the opposite of what your name should do, because almost everyone picks a 'what we do' name. So if you sell phones, everyone's called Phone World, EZ-Tel, Phone King, Mister Phones or Phone Wizard.

Functional names make you another penguin in a vast colony, where your own parents can barely pick you out from the others. When people see your marketing they think it's for the category leader. Other parts of your business will say what you do: your staff, your store, your website. Mediocre marketing comes from staring too closely at any one tactic, as if it was your whole brand rather than one small piece of it.

There is one legitimate use for functional names: niche search-driven naming. Like the plumber who calls himself Riverview Plumbing to win the search results for that suburb. The downside is it's a one-trick strategy that locks you into that niche forever. Okay if you're a sole trader, not great if you want to build something larger.

You can name it after yourself, like Karen Di Angelo Architects. These names work if you never plan to sell your business. Because people will always ask why Karen wasn't on their project. The whole point of a brand is that your business can deliver your values independently of you. Karen Di Angelo Architects is a hard business to sell because so much of the goodwill is tied to one person.

A close relative of this is the Three Initial brand, like JBS Consulting. Short for Jones Business Services or Jackson, Brown and Shapiro or whatever. Those names feel like something you thought up when the accountant called you in the car and said: 'Quick! I need a name for your company, I'm registering it right now.' Really, you have to do better than that.

2. Invented Names

These tend to be either really good or really bad. The good ones are fun to say and stick in your mind. Snapple. Kleenex. Doritos. Though, to be fair, all of those have been hammered into our consciences with billions of advertising dollars over decades.

The bad invented ones use pseudo-Latin roots with a painfully earnest explanation in the press release.

'Announcing Promelior, a new force in personnel recruitment, from the Latin *pro* ('forward') and *melior* ('improve'), boldly symbolic of our passion for engaging the workplaces of tomorrow.'

I made that one up a few years ago as a joke for a presentation. Since then, a real ProMelior opened in the UK, 'Delivering Excellence Through Leadership, Organization and Communications'. There are thousands of these brands. Agilent. Altria. Aquent. They sound like mouthwashes.

3. Evocative Names

The best names are evocative: they make people think of the experience of using your brand, and how that feels. 'Oracle' makes you think of powerful knowledge and seeing into the future. 'Amazon' evokes something vast and unstoppable that penetrates every corner of its territory, and boy did they grow into that. 'Caterpillar' brings a nice personality to all those yellow machines crawling over the landscape on endless tiny feet.

First, get your brand positioning clear. Then get a notebook and write down as many words as you can. Pens find better words than keyboards. Don't think of them as names at this point. Consider your customers and the feelings they get when they use your product. What do they say when they need it? What problems do you solve? What commercial results do they get? What situations lead to them contacting you? Write down *any* words and images that pop into your mind.

Let's run through a couple of examples of how that thought process works.

Inspiration: Bike gang stabbing death

My friend Nic owns an insurance underwriting business that specialises in events – concerts, festivals and sports events. Most of the names in that category are basic functional brands. Insurance Solutions. Concert Cover. Event Underwriting. They all feel the same.

What's on the minds of people planning those events? There's so much scope for traumatic risk. Last-minute cancellations. Weather apocalypse. Temperamental, chemically affected performers. Start writing down words and phrases that might have a name in them.

Box Office? Front Row? Headline? Getting better, but not very inspiring.

Because I'm a music festival tragic, I had a story for Nic. There are few concert tales bigger than the Rolling Stones' 1969 gig to 300,000 people in California. It was total madness. The Stones played on a tiny stage with the crowd pressed right up against it. For whatever reason, the organisation they hired to do concert security was – put this in your green and red grid chart, modern risk assessors – the Hells Angels.

A methed-up punter pulled a gun near the front of the stage. The Hells Angels jumped in and stabbed the guy, who died shortly after. The dazed Stones exited in their helicopter. Three other people died in separate incidents. The name of the raceway where the show was held has passed into legend: Altamont. So that's what Nic named his business, even though he's younger than most of the Stones' children.

Anyone in the concert game knows Altamont, and they respect his nod to this epic yarn. They go: this guy gets our industry. When people don't know it, he has a mighty story to tell them, and they say: *Great name*. And they remember it. Because people have been trained to remember stories since we all sat around cave fires.

Most corporate clients wouldn't choose that name, because it's 'a bit negative'. That doesn't matter. Altamont is a whole biblical morality tale of excess, vanity and madness compressed into *a single word*. 'Insurance Solutions' will never do that.

Inspiration: High Expectations Man

In primitive pre-Tinder times, dating agencies matched couples up for an enormous price. The art of hetero dating services is signing up women. Men follow automatically. The client wanted to appeal to professional women, so we spoke to lots of them.

Their biggest issue was the nightmare first date with High Expectations Man, out to impress. He would arrange a fancy-ass restaurant dinner. If there was no chemistry, which was statistically likely, she was trapped for three courses with an unsuitable man in pleather shoes. The existing dating agencies had a Grand Romance vibe that encouraged this torture.

So we positioned the agency as a no-strings-attached quick catch-up for coffee or a sandwich during gaps in a hectic schedule, so women could make that call fast. Escape was never more than ten minutes away. We named it Pencil You In, with all the executive diary imagery and lack of initial commitment that implied. It grew strongly with only modest advertising; enough to get purchased within a year by one of the other agencies. Sometimes being an annoyance to major players pays off like that.

Evocative names are not always a guaranteed winner. I saw a van in my street branded: Peeping Tom Curtains and Blinds. Tom – if that's your name – *what were you thinking?* Say names out loud. Good names are a pleasure to say, like Snapchat or TikTok. Spell it out loud, like you were giving someone your email address over the phone. If it's a made-up name with letters that sound similar, it will drive you and your staff mad explaining it.

There are free sites that use AI to generate names. I tested some to save you the pain. Our business name, Scene Change, has theatre stage imagery combined with the idea of a fresh start. Could the naming bots do better? I fed them the 'audiovisual' brief, and the first options I got were: Sdiovisual, Pdiovisual, Waudiovisual, and the heinous Videoral. I asked some of our technical crew how they'd feel pulling up to a show in the Videoral truck. No takers there.

When you think of a great name, you'll get excited and picture your new sign above the door. But the naming process is cruel: usually someone's beaten you to it. Do an informal trade mark search on IP Australia's trade mark search site. Trade marks are the brand protection you need, more so than registered business names or company names. There are forty-five classes of products and services. In broad terms, you can use a name if it's not trade marked for your type of product. If the name you love seems free, get a trade mark lawyer to finish the job if you're planning a serious business.

Do a regular web search too. A guitarist I know developed a hardcore range of electric guitar pick-ups, and found a name he felt was perfect. It was, in isolation. It was also the name of one of the world's largest adult entertainment production houses, so he's on about page 37 of search results.

Do you need a tagline? They're hard to do well. For every 'Just Do It', there's a thousand businesses that call themselves '...The Professionals'. Yeah, we get that you're a professional doer of that thing you do, that's why you want money. Then there are those hyper-corporate ones like 'Success. Delivered.' or 'The Power of Certainty' you see in airport ads, underneath stock shots of handshaking suits. They are just public PowerPoint.

A tagline should clarify your brand position. Like 'The Petproof Sofa Store' or 'Insurance For Contractors'. Insurance Nic came up with 'Hope Is Not A Strategy', which I really like.

Aim for human, likeable and not boastful. There's a house for sale in my mum's street. The sign in the front yard has a photo of the agent with her slogan: 'I don't sell homes. I change lives.' *Please.* Just sell the house. There's a clear implication here: 'I am basically the same as charity doctors who restore the sight of African orphans.'

This clueless overstatement of brands' importance in people's lives is why people hate marketing. Your pasta sauce from a jar is not the reason your kids love you. Boasting and exaggeration are no more charming in companies than in people. My current favourite tagline is for the fashion brand Cuyana: 'Fewer, Better Things.' So simple, so good. The antidote to so much mass-produced disposable crap in three words.

ASCENT OF THE
LOGO FASCISTS

It was a logo project for a new boutique bank. Let's call it Classic Bank, for the purposes of this story. My design guy Geoff and I were in their boardroom presenting options for their new brand, plus some ad campaigns. There were three clients there: the CEO, general manager, and a division head.

In the first round of logo presentations, you bring ten designs and cull them. This can get frustrating, as clients instinctively move towards the most conservative suit-blue logo. This went well, though. They narrowed them down to the same two we liked. I suggested they let it settle and make the final choice over the next few days.

'Would it be helpful to get all ten, lay them out on the boardroom table, and get some opinions from the rest of the staff?' asked Matthias, the general manager.

This is never a good plan. It's like trying to get a dozen people at a party to agree on the next song. Commercial sense goes out the window, and random personal fetishes and hang-ups take over.

'No,' I reply. 'There's a time for democracy in business, but for decisions like this sometimes you have to be a little bit . . .'

Matthias is German, an Australian resident for about ten years. Now I know you're thinking: Ian, surely you didn't say 'Nazi' to your nice new German client? No, I kept it to generic dictatorships.

'. . . a little bit fascist about it. You run the company, you know what you want it to become. Trust your own judgement, be strong, and everyone else will just accept it.'

Fascists have run lots of countries – Italy, Spain, Chile. No national stereotyping there. The clients agreed that was a good plan. We moved on to discuss the launch ads. Ten minutes later, Matthias let out a little chuckle.

'You know, Ian, it is funny what you see in things,' he said. 'Since you mentioned the fascist bit before, I've been looking at all the logos, and you know what's really jumping out at me? The "SS" in Classic Bank.'

What? Did I imagine that? Or did he actually say there's a hidden 'SS' in their logo?

'Uh . . . "SS"?' I say, trying to feel out where this was going.

'Yes, they were the paramilitary wing of the German—'

'Um, yes, Matthias . . . we're familiar with their work. But . . . uh . . . I don't think anyone else will notice that.'

The division head leant in and said, 'We'll just have to make sure we pick a logo with nice curvy s's in it.'

'True,' I answer. 'Though the twin lightning bolts served Kiss well, and they're Jewish.'

And the conversation moved on. You go out of your way to not mention the war, and your German client brings in the Schutzstaffel. That one could have gone either way. I ended up working with them for a decade, and Matthias was the most likeable, honorable client I ever worked with. Welcome to the nutty world of logo analysis.

People invest a lot of emotional currency in logos. When big brands change their logos, there's always a storm of indignation from change-haters who preferred the old one. They get really huffy when they read that a new bank logo cost a million dollars. A MILLION DOLLARS! 'I could have done it for *half that*,' comes the predictable response from random punters whose own design skills peaked with a garage sale flyer in Microsoft WordArt.

The reality of large company rebrands is that the million is allocated thus: $25,000 worth of creative work and $975,000 of client meetings where many layers of management say, 'Maybe it's me, but I just don't think it pops,' and 'I don't think orange is relatable.'

You don't have a million dollars, so how do you get yourself a logo? The online world is now full of exciting options to get a new logo for as low as five bucks.

Five bucks.

Think very seriously: if you had to choose a pair of shoes you had to wear to every client meeting for the next ten years, would you spend five bucks? Or seventy-nine bucks? On a purely functional level, you're now equipped to walk around in public. But nobody's going home with you.

Online designers are a very mixed bag. I've spent decades developing design briefs and directing creative people, and I still really struggle with online designers from the big freelancer farms. They rarely read your brief properly, and a lot of their work is first-year design student stuff. I often have to pass the project on to a local designer to fix it.

Part of the trap with most online suppliers is that if you're not a designer yourself, it's tricky to tell good design from bad. It's much like straight male dress sense. We have a limitless capacity to look in the mirror and think: Damn man, you've still got that ol' magic!

People feel cheap-ass design at a subconscious level. They won't be able to give you a forensic reason why, but their animal risk-avoidance instincts scan for signs that businesses are not to be trusted. Or aren't up to the task.

It's not entirely the designer's fault. A major issue is the brief you write for online designers, because that's *all* they have to go on. If you just write the standard brief – *Must have real cut-through! Keep showing me concepts, I'll know what I want when I see it!* – you'll get the same clichés as everyone else.

At a minimum, your brief will need your brand's positioning. Your competitors' logos, so they can design your way out of the crowd. A collection of logos you like. A list of all the applications you'll use it for, apart from the obvious digital and print usage. Video. Packaging. Vehicles. Uniforms. Neon signs. At Scene Change, we need to stencil our logo on roadcases with spray paint. All these things affect your logo.

Plus any weird specifics they should know *before* they do the work, like your phobia about red.

If you want to get the best results out of online designers, here's what I do: make a short list of people whose work you like. Then choose the most expensive designer or coder on that list.

Okay, so that goes against every bit of commercial sense in your lean startup rulebook. Why suggest this madness? Because the expensive ones are still absurdly cheap by any standard. The extra money gets you a pro who understands your brief, follows your checklist, and gets it done fast without you needing to send 200 messages. That is time you should be spending elsewhere.

As an example, my blog website is a WordPress template that cost $79. The coder who set it up with all my menus and content cost $400. He was in my time zone, needed about three messages between the initial brief and launch, and had the site live in less than 48 hours. If I'd chosen one of the many sub-$100 set-up options, I'd have used thousands of dollars of my time checking and explaining. And it would have taken two weeks.

If you can't afford $479 for a website, don't go into business.

There's still no substitute for good designers who work in your city. They can come around, look at your business and products, and talk to you in-depth about what sets your business apart. They'll pick up details you haven't thought of. Their designs will take into account local tastes. No matter how much we become a digital global community, you only have to visit supermarkets in other countries to realise how alien their graphic design can feel. That's what I do on international holidays, because I have poor tourism skills.

The other thing local designers do – maybe the most important thing – is provide continuity. If you use a parade of online designers, you end up with a rat's nest of mixed material pulling the brand in different directions. Rule #1 of brand greatness is consistency. A local designer can grow your design resources as your business evolves, and keep it all clearly part of the same family.

If your budget is super tight, get your local designer to create the overall look, then get the online people to do the tedious hackwork like web banners. The money you spend at the start is nothing compared to the horrifying cost of a rebrand when you realise your successful, mature business has to change your nasty training-wheels startup logo. Redoing all the packaging, stationery, building signs, uniforms and vehicles is a savage cost that could have been avoided by spending a thousand at the start, rather than your dirty fiver deal.

PARTNERS,
OR GO IT ALONE?

How do you structure your new enterprise? You can go it alone. Or
have business partners. I've done both, and the business partner
path is so much more enjoyable. When it's just you, decisions weigh
heavily. You have to make calls on a lot of subjects. Finance. Capex
(capital expenditure). Marketing. Contracts. Staffing. Operations.
Pricing. You are not an expert on all of them – nobody is. Even if you're
Elon Musk, there are entire, vital areas of your business that make you
think: *Ugh, kill me now*.

It's a gift to find business partners you trust, whose skills comple-
ment yours. I'm a marketing and sales kind of guy. I can do operations
and finance, but they bring me no enjoyment and I'm not great at them.

My business partners are, with fine-tuned antennae for the essential
details. Together we have most stuff covered, and as a bonus, we rarely
disagree on anything. Maybe once every two years. Not that constant
agreement is essential or even desirable, but it works for us.

Our mission from the start was to assemble a team of equity partners.
Though Scene Change is a single brand, we set up as separate companies in every location, each with a shareholder running it. They're all
different characters, but each is the sort of person you'd want in your
gang to pull off a glamorous casino heist.

73

The energy is unstoppable. If they saw a sales prospect on the other side of a thistle field, they would run through it in shorts. That mindset flows through to our staff, giving a responsiveness you never get from a head office/branch office business managed by employees. The customers can feel the keen vibe. If we hadn't shared the equity, we would own 100 per cent of a much smaller outfit, because people at our partners' level wouldn't have joined us for just a salary. In most areas they have sharper business skills than me. I'm just the one who likes writing about it.

The other thing the local partners do is balance out what our brand delivers. We do some pretty unusual promotional antics. Generally, our industry enjoys the amusement. But if it was only fun marketing backed up with ordinary technical delivery, it would be a shabby sideshow act. We'd be tricking people into the tent, then disappointing them. People come to us with high expectations. Our staff and partners have the work ethic and technical knowledge to deliver above and beyond. So it's a brand with depth. The idea of a brand that's purely image really creeps me out as a marketer.

Far and away the best part is having a posse. When you have a major win, you want to share that buzz with others who truly understand. They have travelled the whole journey with you, betting everything on making the business work. They have been through all the peaks and troughs along the way. For me, those shared moments are one of the greatest things about owning businesses.

When things turn ugly, you have people you can talk to honestly. Your staff and family sort of get it, but there are things you can't burden them with. Business partners can tell you when you're overreacting and should let issues slide rather than fight every battle. They help you decide how to price that huge new business pitch, whether to move to the bigger office, or to hire that expensive-but-desirable account manager. All the things you agonise over on your own.

If it's just you, you're pretty much Major Tom up there floating alone in your mental spaceship. You had a big win? Have an extra protein pill and pat yourself on the back. Five minutes later, it's back to spaceship maintenance. Got problems? Viewed alone, they get bigger and scarier.

Your paranoia feeds itself, and you can go to some very strange mental places indeed.

You can do whatever the hell you want if the business is all yours. The power is intoxicating. You can cut through the clutter that restrains others and get plenty done fast. But consider how governments work under the same circumstances. Dictatorship is great if you're the one in the stretch Benz, bemedalled jacket and mirrored Aviators. But inevitably, over time and without noticing, you go a bit mad. You lose the discipline of being accountable to others, the western democratic model of business. The discipline of thinking ideas through and persuading others to support your plans leads to better decisions. And you become a better person. You don't start every sentence with 'I', and you don't believe that everything your business achieves is because of you.

Having business partners means someone's checking your progress. That's why some solo startup owners end up working alone at home in a tracksuit, because they spend weeks immersed in choosing the colour of business cards. You need someone to take a stern look at your figures and point out danger. Regularly. Not on your half-yearly visit to the accountant, whose figures reflect ancient history.

Finding good business partners is hard. It's one reason starting a business in your twenties is scary, because you have such limited experience of what people will do long term. Life is all brunch, engagement parties and free time. People change, and for good reasons. Find your business partners later and they've had a chance to have families, or whatever will steer the direction of their life in the long run. They're less likely to reveal they've had a life reassessment and they're off to live without possessions in a yurt in Nepal. This still happens, but with experience it gets easier to predict and manage.

Business skills aside, do you like them? That's essential. If you're considering partnership with someone purely for their massive revenue potential or whatever, but you're not sure if you like them, don't do it. It'll start with passive-aggressive emails, then escalate to screaming matches in the corridor, and you will spend the last of your dwindling cash on barristers. Businesses with the enemy within are a nightmare.

When you choose people to run each location, the most essential characteristic (assuming they have the business skills) is charisma. It's a crowded marketplace and star quality attracts devoted customers and good staff. Your charismatic business partner is constantly bestowing favours and occasionally calling them in, like a Mob boss. They have strong sources of useful information and know exactly what's happening on the street. We've had business partners who didn't work out. It wasn't that people disliked them. It's that people didn't care much one way or another.

Their moral compass is an essential factor. What? Morals? What are you talking about, Ian? What about that old saying about cold-blooded self-interest: *business is business*? Nah. Business involves all sorts of moral judgements, mainly on the question of fucking people over. Sometimes you have make harsh calls, but only when they're deserved. We do not believe in fucking people over. If you have one partner who wants to wring the last cent out of every transaction with clients and staff, and one who wants to build a long-term trustworthy reputation, you're heading for business divorce court.

It's vital to be open about what your endgame goals are. Are you doing it to start and flip, or is this a long-game income caper? Partners need to know. You need a solid shareholder agreement to map out what happens when a partner calls in the Nepalese yurt option.

Get it resolved at the start, while you're all still friends. And if you have decent succession planning, maybe you'll never have to sell the business. That's our plan. Having equity partners is the best way to get yourself away from working in your businesses and know they're being looked after by people who care. More than a decade on, we still regard all our business partners as personal friends, which is some kind of miracle.

THE BEST AGE TO
START A BUSINESS

What's the best age to start a business? When you're aged under thirty, you have no self-doubt. Shades of grey are invisible to you, so you can make decisions much faster. Some of them will be correct, and most of the incorrect ones won't kill anyone.

May I suggest thirty-five for non-tech businesses? I feel sorry for Zuckerberg-style whiz kids (though not the man himself) with the weight of a business on their backs at the age of twenty-three. Owning businesses is a ton of tedious responsibility. Do you want to look back and realise you spent your Friday nights doing your business tax forms, and now you have no friends?

It's a long game. Spend the excellent mid-to-late-twenties period of your life working hard and partying hard, because you can handle both. While making a world of essential educational errors that aren't damaging your own business. When I think of some of the work I did at twenty-five, I just want to run to my car, drive deep into the forest, build a bark hut and see out the rest of my days as a hermit, so there's no chance I'll ever bump into someone who remembers. Get those early screw-ups made on the tab of some big firm that won't miss the money. You'll learn how humans really work, because the textbooks are wrong. You'll meet some future clients, too.

Then you face the big decision. You're killin' it career-wise at thirty-five. Awesome, but know that after the age of forty, you will still have a boss, and you're less tolerant of being told what to do like you're still in school. Sooner or later you'll get a boss younger than you, and she'll be looking at you like, 'How long do I have to keep Miss Daisy here around before I can replace her with someone younger and cheaper?'

The career scrap heap used to be over fifty, which was bad enough. Now it's well into the forties. That leaves you with three or four decades after this to support yourself and your family, when most businesses won't even give you a job interview.

Do you want to wind up your working career with these gnawing insecurities? Staying late just so you can be seen to be working hard? Screw that, you should be working for yourself so you can stay late because it's exciting, and also because you need to. But if your kid has an important school performance or whatever, you can be there because you're now in control of your own time. It's worth having your own business for this benefit alone.

It's not only your kids. Some time after you're forty, your parents are going to need help. It might not happen for a decade or more, but they will have health- or housing-related issues that need you to drop everything and spend time with them.

If you have a full-time job, there is literally no way you can do it. So your parents' needs will have to be subcontracted. And you'll regret it forever, even if your parents made it their life's work to annoy you.

Right now you think this won't happen to you.

It will happen to you.

And it will not happen at the time of your choosing. I've had the freedom to deal with a range of these things, and it is a beautiful and gratifying experience.

Don't get too fixated on thirty-five. If you're forty-five, then that is the best age to start a business. Plenty of people do that successfully. But if you're already thirty, time to start thinking about your escape plan.

Pure digital startups are different. The age is more like twenty-five. There's less to invest. You can live more cheaply. You probably don't have a family. And you might need to start a few businesses and learn from their failure. That takes time. The best way to do it is to start it at night while you're working another job. Side projects – I'm not going to use the h-word – are great. They teach you so much.

Worst-case scenario, even if you never get a business up and running, you will be so much better as a future employee. Creating a new business is like aggressive CrossFit for your brain, giving you skills most can't do at a pro level: product development, branding, packaging, pricing, shipping, cash management, tax, social media and so on.

Smash into that work because they're skills that pay off handsomely later on. You'll give clearer directions, ask the right questions and understand your staff better. When I set up my agency, I did all the books. I learnt how to use the accounting software. I'd sit up late reconciling bank statements and chasing client payments. It wasn't loads of fun, but neither is study or going to the gym. As the perceived 'creative guy', I needed to bulk up the sensible part of the brain that gets the cash through the door.

And puny as it sounds, each month when I did the ordeal of bank reconciliation, seeing the zero pop up to signify balanced accounts was really satisfying. The accountant would tell me the books were in good shape, in the same fashion you compliment your five-year-old on their excellent drawing of a horse.

As the businesses grew, I palmed that job off to bookkeepers and accountants, but now I can understand what they're talking about. Unless you can do that, your business is constantly on the edge. Do the website picture edits. Segment your email database. Pack stuff up for shipping. Learn the tax rulings on full-timers versus casuals.

Later, when you have staff doing those things, you can talk to them as someone who gets it. Rather than the 'How do you do, young person, tell me what tasks you perform here,' Prince Philip style of the clean-hands CEO.

All our business partners pitch in when things get super-busy. They'll go and help unload a truck at midnight. And the conversations they have with our people when they're working side by side are incredibly important for staff morale, and for our understanding of their working lives.

The flip side to all this is making sure you delegate as your business grows. Or you'll end up old, alone and paranoid, afraid that someone might mess up your precious filing system or pay a penny extra for stationery supplies. We've all worked with one of them at some point.

4.

STRATEGY

STRATEGY

GO SOMEWHERE: THAT'S WHERE OPPORTUNITY IS

There's plenty of expert consensus that business travel is dead. It just makes sense. Why on earth would you put yourself through the time, expense and hassle when you can catch up over Zoom? Let me tell you why: to show people you care about them. That's all the justification you need. Not just for karma brownie points, but also to make money.

So much business decision-making assumes anything that saves effort is good. Let's step back and analyse the effort versus reward of digital contact, starting with a friend's birthday. This reminder popped up in my socials: *It's Rob's birthday! Send him good thoughts!* A strong spammy tone, like it came via Google Translate. One click would send him a greeting pre-written by Facebook, and some animated balloons.

That's literally the whole experience.

Seriously, could you put any less effort into a relationship?

You hit a single button like a rat exposed to an experimental stimulus. Job done, the smallest measurable unit of greeting delivered in one second of activity. Even texting 'HBD 🎂' is five times that effort. The birthday person gets a wall of identical pings.

It's not like I always call Rob on his birthday, or frankly even remember it. I'd planned to send a text, but was so repulsed by the

Facebook greeting that I phoned him at work without warning, a direct violation of current etiquette. We talked about crap birthday greetings, and laughed a lot. We resolved to get a drink soon. It felt good.

I'm guessing, if you were a coder, that it would be simple to automate your whole birthday greeting needs forever. Each friend gets a pre-programmed birthday animation, every year until their estimated death age. In the tech-coder mindset, it's so much more efficient, saving you time-consuming single clicks throughout the year.

If your relationship is just an annual click, exactly the same as everyone else's, does that relationship even exist? Why do tech people get to design these features when they clearly have such stunted knowledge of how humans interact? It leads to invented greetings like the LinkedIn work anniversary message, an occasion celebrated by nobody. Or their 'Kudos To You' button. I'm imagining someone in a meeting saying an enthusiastic *Kudos To You, Sarah!* And everyone falling silent and edging away. Then Kudos becomes their embarrass-ing nickname forever.

Tech sells you the dream: we make staying in touch easy and effi-cient! The message your friend or client receives is: you don't care that much. You can present a KPI chart of all the contacts you've made, but you've made nobody feel a thing.

Did we not recently come through a year when we all learnt to dig a bit deeper into how people are feeling, good or bad? That's what relationships are. A one-click transaction is the exact opposite. All the coders involved should be reassigned to productive uses of digital, like helping people buy things more quickly without stupid logins and passwords.

The same effort-to-appreciation ratio applies to your Zoom call to clients or staff. Zoom's great for functional meetings. It's basic box-tick communication, but in no way is it inspirational or special. It's a factory production line of contact. You chat for an hour. Time's up, next. Repeat all day for the rest of your working life. Did you ever get off a Zoom call feeling energised? Or feeling like you had a genius new idea?

When you go to more trouble, people notice. Clients like that you flew there just to catch up. It makes them feel important. There is no other way to build that sense of obligation. If you don't make that effort for your staff, they go into that mindset of 'Everything gets run out of Sydney/Hong Kong/LA or wherever, they're never here and they don't understand what it's like.'

We have tested this. We have businesses in five cities, and we visit them every six weeks. We let that lapse at one point, and we can show you graphs of the performance decline that kicks in after the six-week mark. No report, no Zoom or any other remote observation method works. You must go, physically.

Overnight visits work best. Fly in and out in one day and it's like a prime ministerial media visit. Lots of shaking hands, nodding, people smiling and showing you nice, sanitised, pre-prepared things. It's all facade, no reality. Spend more time around the office and people relax. They become used to your presence, like you're shooting a nature documentary. You're not trying to entrap them; it's fairer to observe things when they're not trying to put on a show. You get a sense of how they work, how they talk to each other, what layers of respect and hierarchy operate. You have to go out to dinner with the local manager and let them relax. This is when they say what's really on their mind.

The physical appearance of your business holds important clues. During one of our non-visiting periods, we noticed the profitability of one office on a sharp decline. The P&L (profit and loss statement) said skyrocketing labour costs. But why? We visited, and there were big new desks everywhere. Each with two monitors. And comfy chairs. Because some of the technical staff had promoted themselves into operations management positions, mostly involving 'researching new technology', aka sitting on their arses browsing the web.

We discussed it on the flight home. My idea was to make our next visit to that office unannounced, with a crew of enormous tattooed removalists. They would pick up the extra desks – 'Excuse me, bro, do you mind if I just grab that?' – smash them into matchsticks, and dump the wreckage in a skip outside. These are the kind of incidents company mythology is made of. Peter rightly pointed out that this was a lunatic idea. This is one reason why having business partners is a good idea.

We flew back a couple of weeks later for a very stern group talking-to, another thing that doesn't work at all over Zoom. The Comfy Chair Index remains a sure measure of the health of the business. Every business has these off-the-books indicators that your accountant will never be able to explain. After a while, you can smell them the moment you walk through the door.

If you're doing everything virtually now, your spider senses are not developing. They'll remain frozen at the time you stopped the face-to-face contact. What separates good from great business people is mainly instinct. Decades of conversations, calculations and analysis get hard-coded in, to the point where you don't need a spreadsheet. You just know. And you'll never know if you never go.

I'm desperate to go again. I love airports. I love their sense of infinite possibility. They're a vast concrete reminder that you can go anywhere you like and create something new. Departure boards scroll through endless exotic destinations. Herds of busy people swarm past, on their way to turn the wheels of commerce and make interesting shit happen. You and I are incredibly lucky to have been born in an era where we can just go and have adventures and do deals, transported in a comfy sky chair with free drinks. Rather than a six-month voyage in a tea clipper with pirates on the horizon.

I watch the planes and the people, and I feed off that energy. Let's go and *make something happen*. That's why I love going to America. Despite the poison coffee, the sheer scale of the place makes me realise whatever I've achieved is small and I need to do better. I revise my goals, read more books and lift my game. Every trip pays for itself.

None of this happens with Zoom calls. Your horizons narrow rather than expand. It's a sort of digital glaucoma. A shrinkage of your epic vision so gradual you don't notice, until all you see is what's right in front of you. And I think Zoom will forever be associated with a survival mentality, from those grim bunkered-down chats of 2020. Our subconscious mind sees the Zoom screen and stays in the cave. No swashbuckling, world-conquering drive, just the safe cocoon of home.

Business is not about doing what everyone else is doing. It's about doing something different to your competitors, duh. Going places will be a competitive edge. I'm also willing to bet that being well-dressed will be a business superpower over the next few years, while everyone else looks like a tramp. Tramp casual is a cool reverse flex if you own Atlassian. The rest of you: dress the fuck up and leave your homes.

REMOTE WORK SUCKS
UNLESS YOU'RE OLD

Right now, lots of people are writing think-pieces called 'The end of the office?' Remote work will take over, say futurists.

No, it won't. It's great for a few days a week, and for some people at certain stages of their lives. But if you keep everyone remote working full-time, in a couple of years you'll have an ominous skills black hole. If you're older and experienced, remote working is fine. You're comfortable with the territory. You have contacts if you need advice or support, people you met back in the physical world. Your younger staff will do their best, but they only have their family, housemates and the UberEats rider to learn from.

When you're starting out, the training value of having experienced people around you all day is huge. They answer questions. They take you aside and suggest how you might handle that situation better next time. Even if they say nothing, watching and listening is everything. Yes, there's Zoom. But it's how people behave when they're *not* on show that provides the deep-down lessons. You learn by how people deal with chaos. How they treat other people all day. How they act in meetings when they're *not* talking. How they handle disagreement. A person being a dick by ignoring everyone all day after an argument doesn't show up on Zoom. One more essential conflict-resolution lesson that never happens.

No business has a future if you cut off the pipeline of quality up-and-comers, and having physical premises will be a competitive selling point for great young staff. They want to learn. They want fun. They want to compete with others on their level, and they want to go out afterwards. Not log off, turn around and see their parents on the couch.

Young workers have the worst work-at-home options. Comfortable managers tend to assume all workers have a nice spare room at home like they do, with a curated bookshelf background. If you're twenty-three and living in a share house, a spare room doubles your rent. Who's paying for that? There's noise, distractions and bandwidth competition from gamer housemates. Share houses are even worse than offices for passive-aggressive fridge notes about not drinking *my* oat milk.

Getting people together is a vital culture builder when you're starting a business. In those early days, you're laying down the foundation of what your brand stands for. The interpersonal chat *between* the formal conversations and meetings is the morale glue that holds your gang together. Nobody in a remote work team will Zoom each other to talk about their family, hobbies, pets or weekend antics. Everyone remains a two-dimensional screen image. So in tough situations, they don't really have each other's backs, like they would with work friends that sit together all day.

Remote work drains people's batteries long term. Founders and senior managers tend to believe everyone thinks like them, obsessing about the business all the time. Most people aren't, and don't want to. They have . . . lives. When they work at home, particularly with kids present, they're distracted and guilty about not getting through enough work during the day. After hours, it still feels like they're at work, so they feel guilty they're not present with their family. Most people like that separation. Without it, the mental fatigue ratchets up. That staleness reflects in their work. Bad for them, and bad for your business.

Something else to consider if you work for a big company: getting the whole job done from home is a reminder that they could replace you with someone else in a lower-paid country. You know they'd do it in a heartbeat. It won't happen this year, but give it two years and a consulting firm report, and you're a 'cost disadvantage' to them. Start thinking how you can re-establish a physical presence in the business, or you're a target.

There's another drawback to remote work, though this isn't the book for relationship advice. Prediction: full-time remote work will create a massive spike in divorces and separations in a couple of years.

Because one or both of you will be bored out of your mind with the other. You have no conversation topics other than domestic duties. There is no news. There are no surprises. You are not interested in hearing about their day, because you were right there at the scene. You know what happened. Zoom calls, two Nespresso flat whites and a toasted sandwich. Every. Fucking. Day.

There are no interesting stories about the political battles, the office affairs, the underhand plots, the villains and heroes of work world. These tales are all the better if your partner doesn't know the people involved, because they become cartoon characters in the retelling, with exaggerated strengths and defects. It's really entertaining.

Don't tell me you're above all that 'gossip'. It's basic Shakespeare. People have lapped it up since the dawn of time. Rule: it's not gossip if it's just you and your partner talking about it. It's only if it leaves the house. Particularly if it comes up at the office Christmas party. 'Oh, *you're* the one who . . .' Then you both have to leave fast.

There was the first period of home-office bliss, the extra sleep-in and the freedom from workplace stress. Both of you dressed in the Zoom mullet: business at the top, leisure below the desk. You get to a point where even jeans feel harsh after so long in tracksuit pants. How good is this compared to office life? So much less effort.

As with your client relationships, you forget that effort was what created the attraction in the first place. Pure animal kingdom signalling. Now you're wearing drab plumage that says you just don't care anymore. Some relationships are fine with that. But you never know if you're permanently fine.

Sooner or later, one of you is going to crave some excitement. It doesn't have to be swingers clubs or opening an Ashley Madison account. It might just be a coffee with someone who looks at you in a way that says: I'm interested in this conversation. That can be all it takes. Chemicals kick in and it's life reassessment time.

Boredom might not be the thing that gets you. It's also the feeling of being trapped. Because when one of you leaves the house, it's 'Where are you going?' and 'For how long?' These questions start as natural, if unimaginative, chat. Then, when one of you is in a mood, it starts to feel like surveillance. It builds from there. You have nothing that's your own.

Couples who use phone trackers on each other start off like it's a friendly convenience. Then it's 'I see you're at the shops, how much longer are you going to be?' then 'What were you doing at Andy and Marsha's place?' There's a fine line between sharing everything and 24/7 control that will drive one of you mad and ignite burning resentment.

All this could be solved with seeing less of each other and an understanding that a bit of mystery is a good thing. Nobody is so attractive that you want to be with them all day, every day. One of you, get back to commuting before it's too late.

THE HAIRDRYER
HORROR SHOW

The worst thing about being trapped in a corporate bubble is that you don't know it. Sure, you might often be right. But sometimes you won't. The citizens of Customerland aren't you. Their lives are different. They will do things you wouldn't have dreamed of doing without powerful hallucinogens.

Consider my gym, which was renovated a few years back. It used to be a classic old sports club gym, full of retired football players with hairy necks. Then they updated it with gleaming machines, buff trainers and deluxe hotel-style change rooms. In those change rooms, next to each basin, were hairdryers attached to the bench.

Not long after the renovation, I noticed one of the older chaps at the mirror blow-drying his armpits. Nude. Really, sir, isn't towel-drying dry enough? Things escalated. Moving into a deadlift-style semi squat, he dropped the dryer to knee level, pointed it upward, and dried his ancient dangling genitalia, eyes shut, a faint smile on his face.

I'm fairly sure that when the architect designed the new facilities, they didn't imagine that application. And old mate wasn't the only one doing it. It's A Thing with old men, along with talcum powder. Apparently, as you get older, you get a powerful hankering for total dryness. If you're a younger person marketing to older people, you need to know these peculiarities. Even if you're personally okay with a bit of moisture in your crevices post-shower.

Most people think growing old is a gradual phase, a decades-long slowing of vital functions as the youthful chemicals fizzle out, replaced by an urge to move to places where you can wear shorts all year and eat at 6 pm. It's not. 'Old' is a binary, yes/no state that happens in an instant transformation, like becoming a werewolf. All your life, you refer to air moving around by names like 'wind', 'breeze', 'ventilation' and similar pleasant words. That's a refreshing afternoon breeze, you think, enjoying the gentle tingle of air on skin. Then one day it happens. You use the word 'draught'. 'Can you feel a draught?' Pow! You've become an Old Person right there.

From that moment, life becomes a mission to block the nightmare air movement of the outside world. 'Shut that damn door!' It's like the medieval belief that illness comes from bad vapours. 'You'll catch your death.' In his old age, my dad became a sort of landlocked submarine commander, bolting the doors and windows of their intensely humid, flat-iron-roofed home in the subtropics, keeping the demon draughts at bay.

As a business person, if you don't understand different perspectives to your own, you're doomed to sell to your own tribe only. It's important even in the way you sell ideas to your own staff in meetings. I often wonder how any woman who has been through childbirth feels when asked to 'man up' for some modest business challenge. Or how ex-military people who have actually been shot at enjoy hearing sales managers declaring: 'It's war out there.'

Friend bubbles also lead you astray. Your chat group is all people like you. It might start as a throwaway line to show that you're part of the cool gang, not like the stupid dirty public. Like 'Nobody watches TV anymore.' Say it often enough and you start saying it in meetings like it's data, rather than your description of your own reflection.

After seeing the hair dryer thing for the fifth time, I couldn't resist asking the front desk woman if there was anything they could do. I described the scene and watched the colour drain from her face.

'He did . . . WHAT?!'

It would have been an interesting agenda item for their next staff meeting, as a gang of fit, perky twenty-somethings came to grips with behaviour light years outside their universe. Your customers do stuff you can't comprehend. People taste pet food to make sure it's good enough for their precious fur baby. They use sports betting apps at the table when they're out to dinner with their partner. Exercise equipment makers should visit hotel gyms: bizarre workout circuses where people sit on machines backwards and use free-weight techniques they saw in *Popeye* cartoons.

The more you get out of your office and observe customers, the more amazing, and useful, stuff you will learn. And the more you learn to speak their language, because that's the best way to win their trust. When I was writing TV ads for my tyre client, our strategy was to target women, who were mostly disgusted by tyre stores. I'd go to an outer-suburban shopping mall and sit in the food court for an hour or so, just listening and tuning in to conversations. Then I'd pull out the notebook and start writing. It was always productive. These people aren't interested in your hipster ad-writer wordplay. They have bills to pay and screaming kids to wrangle. It clarifies your thinking and teaches you not to waste their precious time.

These observation skills are essential in sales. Listen to the words your clients use. Every industry has code words and acronyms. People in travel talk like this: 'The client's PCO says they've got 500 pax in a MICE group, plus some FITs from LAX. Can the DMC reps arrange a famil ASAP?' Outsiders go: WTF. Listen to what your clients say and use *their* words back to them. They subconsciously think: *at last, someone who speaks our language*. So they trust you.

On the flip side, beware of inflicting your own industry jargon on outsiders. For example, take the industry that moves things in trucks from one place to another. It used to be called freight. Everyone knew what freight was. Then marketing people got involved and it became logistics, because that sounded less working-class. Then, over many brainstorms, it got broadened to Integrated Logistics.

Next brainstorming meeting: 'I know! What about Total Integrated Logistics Solutions?' says some keen contributor. 'That's gold! Take a photo of the whiteboard, we're done!'

The hairdryer horror show

So the trucks outside my local supermarket say Total Integrated Logistics Solutions. That's a lot of words so it shrinks to the acronym. TILS, pronounced 'tills'. Everyone in meetings now says 'tills', till 'tills' sounds normal. To them. They start saying it to customers and people at barbecues. Then come marketing masterstrokes like 'TILS without the spills', as if that makes sense to anyone outside their oxygen-starved PowerPoint bunker.

This lack of awareness can lead you to say some strange stuff. I had a visit from a mailing house rep. Mailing houses call themselves 'fulfilment' now. Their man was a classic confident sales guy with the electric-blue suit, Premier League haircut, and a general sense you could catch chlamydia just by clicking on his LinkedIn invitation.

His company offered two services: classic bulk postage, or sending larger marketing packages that needed hand-assembly. He was particularly proud of their manual work.

'Hand fulfilment is our specialty,' he said with a winning smile. I'll pass on that, thank you. Try to step back and consider how your patter sounds to normal humans.

DISRUPTION WARS: YOU VERSUS THE KILLER ROBOTS

So, you've mapped out your lucrative niche, but how long will it last? Could it be redundant in five years? It's tricky to predict, given the number of business 'futurists' who get paid in the present for their keynote speech, long before their flaky predictions can be fact-checked.

It seems cruel that some of the industries hit hardest by COVID-19 were already on their knees from tech disruption. Travel agencies were already shaky before international travel shut down. Music industry fortunes had already dropped from Merck pharmaceutical-grade cocaine to Aldi nangs after CDs left the scene. Then the virus tried to kill live music, their last source of cash.

Who's next for the chop? How do you stop the AI invasion from replacing you and your soft, carbon-based staff? Other than by rehearsing the line: 'I, for one, welcome our new robot overlords'? One answer is in the haphazard analog glory of human behaviour. Now is not the time to be too close to your own product. Think about what you really provide. Beyond your product's function, what excitement, risk reduction, time saving, convenience, social interaction or flexibility do you deliver?

Let's pick a business: bars and pubs. What do they provide? Drinks, obviously. If all-out tech replacement was the answer, bars would have no staff. Just a self-serve ordering app and robot drink-dispensing tech that already exists. And what a grim fucking night out that would be.

It's then you realise that bars provide a sense of community. Staff who can broaden your knowledge of cocktails, and make you feel important by recognising you. For some, those staff might be the only people who ask them how their day was. There's the anticipation that tonight's drinks might become an occasion of some sort, rather than pure consumption. The sort of bar you go to is a badge of your personality. So is your choice of drink. Some of us are plush furnishings people; I'm a bit of a sticky carpet guy. Any objective cost–benefit analysis would recommend that you have those drinks at home on the couch. Like a loser finance analyst. You can't fight robots with logic.

The traditional and still popular approach to business is to develop a bulletproof process that you can scale. So management becomes a task of machine-like adherence to the rule book. Variations are measured and logged. Errors are punished. If you program your staff to behave like machines, why would you be surprised when a new competitor replaces them with software?

I'm an optimist, and not super-worried that AI will destroy all our jobs. There will be new jobs. But I have absolute faith in the big business ability to take new technology and create an annoying experience: big business can't resist the awesome cost-cutting features. This is your chance to stand out from their robot army. Give your staff the freedom and the skills to step outside the flow chart when *it doesn't matter*. Because lots of processes are written for the lowest common denominator. Applying them uniformly to all your customers sends a message: *you are no different from our worst, stupidest customer ever.*

Here's one thought: *let your frontline people break the rules when it doesn't matter*. This is an area where Australians have a cultural advantage. We're up for it more than others. It's an opportunity for your small, flexible business.

You can't break the rules all the time, or your business will be a total monkey house and you'll lose money. But only a human will ever be able to look someone in the eye and make an exception to the system. It's the judgement call that makes that moment more convenient, and that's what makes your customer feel like an individual. Hire the sort of people who will look at the mother struggling with shrieking kids on a wet day and go: 'I'm going to cut you a break here.' She will tell others.

Your staff become experienced judges in the Court of Customer Service, with the wisdom to know when to go lenient, and when to hand down zero-tolerance to scammers. While your cost-cutting competitors become more like US airport security, crushing customer spirits with no-exceptions process reinforced by ever-more-intrusive technology.

The bigger theme is a decline of responsibility in business. If you have a face-to-face conversation with a person, that person will take some sort of responsibility. They're less likely to go back on their promises, and they can be held accountable.

Accountability is harder to find each year. Go to the contact page of any big company website now, and good luck finding a phone number. You'll need a Dark Web browser for that. Even if big companies aren't completely replacing human contact, they never add *more* service. Their cost-cutting only goes one way. Fewer people. Less responsibility. At the end of 2020, Qantas announced it was ending airport service counters, instead providing 'self-serve recovery' for lost luggage. 'Find your own damn bags.' If you tried to custom-design a system to enrage tired customers, you couldn't top that.

Everyone focuses on Apple's nifty product design and branding as the foundation of its success. But their huge, underrated benefit is that when stuff ain't working, you can always talk to someone who cares and is committed to fixing it.

I heard someone spruiking a 'disruptive' financial planning service which keeps fees low with 'advanced software that saves on the expense of staff and branch offices'. Translation: you'll be trapped in an AI rat maze designed to block your quest for human help. This isn't buying a t-shirt. This is the management of your life savings, and they want you to trust the machines all the way. When, inevitably, there is trouble, nobody is there to hear your story. 'Please, tell Ms Perky Chatbot your long history of service nightmares for the third time, after the beep.'

If that advisory firm gets into financial trouble, where do you go? Who do you call? Without offices, old-school though they may be, how do we know it's not just a super-professional, long-game Russian hacker scam?

The guy who does our digital campaigns had another of his clients, a digital store, shut down by Google, 'because it doesn't comply with our Program Policies'. Despite being a digital super-soldier, he can't work out why. Google's template email continues:

'This enforcement is completely automatic in nature and hence, we or even the specialist team cannot pinpoint the exact policy reason that led to account suspension.'

Then a link to a gigantic archive of policy rules. How do you like the idea of unaccountable AI shutting your business? While the AI's human owner goes: 'Hey *shrug emoji* we can't control it'?

Plenty of people are prepared to pay over the odds to avoid this dystopian anti-service future. Time is money. Or, for working mothers, time is a distant memory. If you can save people from being dicked around for hours, they're interested. It's never been so important that your people remember those customer conversations and promises, and deliver on them.

Digital experience designers are getting better at faking the human touch with customer service avatars and the like, but people still instinctively know they're dealing with code, and that's okay. Customers are fine with code for routine transactions. Build your business advantage around the non-routine, and find the gaps robots can't get through. They will always exist.

Never forget Hairdresser Syndrome. So many people live with bad hair, thanks to the fear that if they dump their hairdresser, they will run into them in the street one day and have to explain why they don't go there anymore.

Replace that frontline human touch with automation, and from an emotional viewpoint, you're just a vending machine. Digital is exciting, but it's not the only thing. It's important not to lose track of the value of the tangible world, the world of cuddles and warm water lapping on your feet and the smell of babies and the glorious sensation of drinking champagne in airport departure lounges at 8 am because you're going on holidays and nobody can tell you what to do.

These are the things that make people feel good; moments that they want to last forever, things that they want to tell their friends about. Massive as social media is, without real experiences to fill up the timeline, it would be nothing but your uncle's racist memes about the proposed neighbourhood mosque.

What will your business do to make reality a little bit better for people? What human touches are you building into your approach to keep those robots at bay? Go digital to cut costs and streamline process where it doesn't affect service, and add more humans where their presence will set you apart.

Obviously, if your exciting idea is an app, you can ignore all this love-and-hugs stuff. A friend sells his project management app into large corporations and he tells them straight up: 'This app will allow you to make a load of people unemployed.' Their faces light up when they hear it. You might be working for those people right now.

SECRETS OF SERVICE BUSINESSES: LIKEABLE BEATS SKILFUL

As a lifelong marketing guy, I wish I could say marketing is the biggest secret to building service businesses. Sadly for my self-esteem, it's not. Referrals and word-of-mouth outweigh everything else. Your search word campaigns bring in comparison shoppers, which is useful but hard work. If you're on a small business budget, ads usually attract . . . not much at all. New business sales calls are an endless grind.

Referrals do what you can't: they say you're great. If you say 'We're great!' in your own marketing, it's lost in all the other self-basting businesses saying the same thing. Customers just assume it to be a lie anyway. People who have been referred to you turn up on your doorstep, pre-sold by one of your other lovely clients, expecting you to be good.

So where do referrals come from? From you being the best? Not really. Think about your own purchasing habits. Could you recommend a good motor mechanic or accountant? Or some other service person you've recommended before? Let's say it's your accountant. How up to date is she with changes to retirement tax laws? Or home office asset depreciation? How are her Excel skills?

You have no idea. You don't know how good your car mechanic, accountant or dentist are. The whole reason you need them is because you don't understand what they do. You can't rank your mechanic's skills accurately against the entire population of mechanics. So choosing a service supplier is a two-step process.

Step 1: Are they basically up to it?

You don't know if they're the best, but you know they're good enough. They have certificates. They've done nothing to make you doubt their competence. They usually get it done on time, and that's often your only objective measure of their skill.

That's good enough to proceed to Step 2. They could improve their skills another 47 per cent through professional development, and you wouldn't notice. Good enough is good enough. But they won't get referred unless they pass the final test.

Step 2: Do you like them?

Do you feel they understand you? Are they pleasant to work with? Do they remember little details about you? Are they interested in what you're trying to achieve? Do they keep you informed if something's running late or going wrong? When they make a mistake – which everyone does – do they own it honestly and quickly?

These are the building blocks of likeability. If you like them, then they are a great accountant. So you'll use them forever. And you'll refer them to your friends.

This is how you build any service business. An hour spent getting to know your client better is generally more productive than an hour spent making yourself technically better at your job. Ask. Listen. Remember. Don't talk over them.

Likeability is even more important now. Clients can stalk you on your socials, so you have no secrets. If you're under thirty, you'll find it hard to imagine the pre-smartphone firewall that separated Corporate You and Personal You. Personal You had to be kept closeted. Employers put lots of effort into making Corporate You more businesslike. It was like living in stock photo world: all ties, skirt-suits and handshakes around boardroom tables with fat grey laptops.

Some friends started their first accounting jobs with doomed global firm Arthur Andersen. As you might expect of a firm named Arthur, it was a pretty stuffy place. They sent the newbies to a How-To-Dress course. On weekends you're still representing the firm, they were told, so lose the jeans and shorts and consider 'chinos and a blazer'. I'm not sure what they told women to wear, but the general idea was to create a generation of young golf club fogeys. Best of all was the weekday styling advice: men, wear striped ties, and make sure the stripes rise from left to right, 'like a rising graph'. All those friends left accountancy, and no wonder.

Remember that half of being likeable is not being dislikeable. Don't assume everyone is the same as you. A supplier of ours opens most conversations with insulting references to one side of politics, on the assumption that because we are business people, we're on the other side. Maybe we are, maybe we aren't. My politics are of no interest to you, but it's dangerous to assume everyone's on your team when roughly half the population isn't.

There's a balance here. I'm not suggesting you stop bothering to lift your skills. Professional pride should keep you doing that. Like-ability without skill will build you a house of cards that will collapse at some point.

Just don't take it personally when clients don't notice the finer details of your genius skills, because they're simply invisible to them. This is what makes technical experts tell their sales team: 'We really need to educate these customers.' Translation: *We want everyone to share our maniacal obsessions.* That ain't going to happen, and it's perfectly okay.

You'll build a bigger business by remembering people's names. The rules of making people like you haven't really changed since the cave days, and Dale Carnegie nailed the topic in 1936 with *How To Win Friends and Influence People.* Most biz books since then have just been a rehash of his work. The book is wordier and more man-centric than today's books, but it's well worth reading to remind yourself that some business truths are timeless.

BUSINESS WHACK-A-MOLE SKILLS

In business you need a polar mindset combo of crazed optimism and practical pessimism. Without both, your business will die. You need the optimism to keep the whole show on the road. From the start, I've never had a millisecond's doubt that our businesses would work, and that becomes self-fulfilling. And you need pessimism because you must be ready for the bad things that pop up with whack-a-mole frequency.

Some business people seem amazed to see those moles. I heard a radio interview with a winemaker facing a huge revenue drop because China is annoyed with Australia, so now they've started import bans.

Wine man is irate because 'It's the government's fault', and 'It's their responsibility to find us new markets.' Imagine having a business that entirely relies on eternal perfect relations with a communist government, and thinking: *everything's fine*. Despite the Hong Kong chaos, US–China trade wars, and global diplomatic battles over the COVID-19 origin inquiry. That or he's been so deep in wine work he hasn't bothered checking what his biggest client is up to, even though it's conveniently served up on the evening news. Either way he's thought: *no need to act, and if things turn bad, the government must step in to be our export sales department.*

Guess which legendary region his wines are from? Yes, the Gold Coast.

If you can't deal with risks any clown could have seen coming, how are you going to cope when a single tasty pangolin dinner spawns a world-stopping virus? Our business survived COVID-19 because we were pessimistic in 2019. We'd expected an economic downturn, because they happen every decade or so. All the indicators were there, like overvalued share markets and house prices. Rather than pull all the profits out of the business, we reinvested in income-producing things. When the downturn came, we were ready to push through, while others took a cash-flow pounding.

We had diversified our client base so that the loss of one big client couldn't kill us. That's a major risk to so many businesses. Client change is real. You can do the best job in the world, and you can still lose the client for reasons outside your control. Your contact changes companies or gets promoted out of that role. They stop needing what you provide, or their business gets sold. If you depend on one or two big clients, you're in the danger zone.

This is a good moment to put a classic motivator story in the bin. It's the one where the army burns their boats on the shore. So as to rule out the possibility of retreat. Alexander the Great did it. Hernán Cortés also. Sun Tzu recommends it in *The Art of War*.

'Now that's commitment!' says the keynote speaker. 'Would they have conquered those lands if they had a convenient fallback position? No! That's how real leaders commit!'

Yes, this brave bro-talk *is* commitment. It is also terrible risk management from people who will destroy your business like boats on a beach. YOU ARE NOT IN A LITERAL WAR. You are most likely tapping away at a laptop in the seated position, and that is not the same as being speared or shot.

Remember how Envato started its life as FlashDen, a purely Flash marketplace? Collis started some some side projects with blog themes and music tracks. Advisers felt they were a distraction.

'People told us, "Flash is a goldmine, just focus on beating your Flash competitors,"' Cyan said.

Then Steve Jobs publicly declared war on Flash, and banned it from Apple's mobile devices. From that moment, Flash was dead in the water. Envato sailed on to glory in their spare boats.

If you can't motivate yourself for a project without first cutting off all your other options, business is not your thing. I've known a few people who love this hero posturing: 'I'll show them!', 'That'll teach them!', and so on. Long term, they're great at burning things. But not great at consistently building wealth, happiness or much else.

Your balance sheet is the clearest measure of how much trauma you can withstand (more on that later). That's what got us through. In 2020, the virus arrived, and our income went down to zero for three months.

The TV cameras we'd bought the year before saved us. We built virtual TV studios in our now-idle warehouse space, for clients who wanted something better than drab home-office Zoom. We dumped our whole website and made a new one in two weeks, selling us as a studio business. We created training programs to help execs present to camera in this strange, no-visible-audience environment. By the end of the year, even with the studios busy, we were still at 40 per cent of normal monthly revenue. COVID-19 *did* kill our single largest client.

But we will survive, thanks to our paranoid, survivalist mindset. Always expect bad things. And if they don't happen, happy days.

5.

MARKETING & SALES

COLOURING IN
FOR GROWN-UPS

If you want your new business to become a brand, you have to start from day one. A brand is not some bolt-on accessory you can add later. Investing the time and money to create a brand can go against your rational business instincts. It's a bit of a tribal clash. On one side are the brand evangelists, quoting from the Book of St Jobs on the sparkling wonders of creativity, your only competitive edge in the grey world of business.

On the other, business people view creative marketing as colouring-in for grown-ups, delivered by pretentious freaks who say, 'Mandrill Orange is so on point right now, it's the PMS Colour of the Year.' Most creatives can't explain how this magical colour, or anything else in their hipster toolbox, will actually bring money through the door.

I've been on both teams and both are right and wrong. One of the reasons Scene Change exists is because of my frustration at having good marketing ideas killed by hyper-cautious clients. Yes, they were creative ideas, though not indulgent. They were all designed to meet strict commercial goals, but it's an uphill battle. You see so many consultants spruiking creativity to big companies, believing it's inarguably good. But creativity is feared and persecuted to the highest levels in most large businesses, despite all the 'committed to innovation' mission statement schtick. What they want is manageable conformity.

'We really loved the ideas, they're so . . . creative! We just felt now is not the right time for them.'

By 'creative' they mean: 'Your ideas make us uncomfortable; our boss will hate them a lot, so we won't risk our careers by supporting them.'

Scene Change became a test lab for the sorts of ideas I spent a decade having euthanised. My business partners and I bet our houses, cars and pets on these madcap ideas working. If it didn't strike a chord with customers, our next job would be on the footpath, wearing sandwich boards advertising early-bird parking.

In terms of turning random notebook scrawls into cash, these experiments worked very nicely. Sometimes I'll tell Peter I've had an idea and he'll just say, 'Don't even tell me what it is, surprise me.' We launched our own beer and cider brand purely as a promotional exercise. We invested in a private jet so we could park it on the runway at Hamilton Island airport, because our entire industry had to walk past it when they arrived for a conference, creating a hilarious word-of-mouth inferno.

We invited a group of our competitors to join an industry band, AV/DC, to play the conference after-party. As a brand experience, it's quite the buzz to play for a hyped-up audience of 350 delegates in a dark bar, most of them wearing the 'At the back, in black' band t-shirts we gave them. It works a lot better than what everyone else does: a plodding 'leave your business card and win an iPad' contest. Five years later, people still ask when we're playing again. We weren't *that* good but fun gets remembered.

Do we know all these capers are going to work? No. Some don't. It doesn't bother us. Some campaigns work better than you hoped, and it all averages out. If anyone tells you they can accurately predict if a marketing initiative will work, they are a straight-up liar. Just keep doing things that consistently fit your company personality, and over time the cumulative effect is unstoppable. This is the Darwinian advantage of your smaller business: you can do whatever the hell you like. Your staff and clients are drawn to your sense of exhilaration.

The other great thing about your own business is that you can apply your ideas across everything you do, not just the narrow scope of promotions. When I did client campaigns, it got frustrating knowing any customer enquiry would hit a wall of shabby stores or indifferent staff with tobacco breath. In your own place you have the power to make everything fit the image you created. How can you turn every interaction with customers into an 'ad' that makes them want to use you more?

There's a theory that half your marketing investment works to reassure existing clients that they've made the right choice. I'd agree, but would take this further. If our marketing won us zero new clients, we'd still do it, because our staff dig it. It makes them feel like they're part of something more interesting than other places. They're proud of it, it shows in their work, and the business sells itself.

I can see how business owners get frustrated with branding people, though. Branding people do care about making your business a success, but sometimes their lack of hands-on business experience shows. Google 'How to create a winning brand', or go to conferences on that topic, and a thousand brand 'gurus' tell you to be more like the ultimate brand: Apple. The beautiful products! The cool stores! The packaging! The ads!

Which is great, except you are not Apple and never will be. It's the richest company on earth, and employed creative geniuses like design wizard Jony Ive. You can't do that, and if you come back from a seminar determined to be more Apple, the immense pressure will cause you to do nothing. Saying 'Be more Apple' is like that point in an argument when you call your opponent 'Hitler'.

Apple just reaches into its bottomless money pit to pay for the brand magic that becomes conference case studies. But most marketing people have to beg for money from a flint-hearted finance creep with zero interest in your talk of 'brand values' or making your company 'cool'. You may as well talk to your teenage child about superannuation.

So from a cold self-interest perspective, here's why you need a brand. A brand is all that stops you needing to be the cheapest of six quotes. Why is that? Because a brand offers reassurance and lower risk. Customer confidence is a timid fawn, easily spooked by surprises and sudden movement. Brands are the antidote to the 'change fear' we spoke of before.

This is especially true for business-to-business companies. See it from your customer's perspective. If they achieve greatness in their corporate project, they get a pat on the head and perhaps an Employee of the Month certificate. Contrast that with the sledgehammer punishment of the screw-up. Double that for government customers. When the punishment of errors outweighs the rewards of greatness, your brand is there to reassure potential customers it's all going to be okay. Your customers feel safe among the herd of others who use you.

Without a brand, price is all you've got. So it's always tough. You know those business people who say: 'I've never seen it so tough out there'? All the time I've been in business the same people have been saying it.

'Compared to when?' I ask. 'Oh, ten years ago it was so much better,' they say. Believe me, they were complaining ten years ago and pining for the good times ten years *before that*. The common factor all this time has been: them. The whole 'good old days' mindset is a problem.

In tough times, the first urge of business people is to cut costs, and rightly so. And the first cuts are usually the touchy-feely intangibles in the marketing budget. So margins decline. Which means investment decisions get delayed, which demotivates staff, sending them hunting for a better job. You lose your good people, which costs you clients. You cut more costs and the cycle repeats: a downward spiral into business hell.

If you have a solid brand, it's the opposite. You have higher margins so you make more profit. You can afford to reinvest more. This means company growth, and career growth for your people. Your staff feel like they're on a righteous mission, and everyday working life feels great. You can afford nicer rewards for high-performing staff. The sense of building momentum is intoxicating.

But wait, there's more. Let's talk about pure profit benefits. Staff is the biggest expense of most businesses. If you have a strong brand, good people want to work for you. And you can hire them for what crap companies pay for plodders. It becomes self-perpetuating, as good staff attract more people like them.

We spend no more than 2 per cent of turnover on marketing. That's pretty modest. Staff turnover costs most businesses much more in recruitment, training, getting new staff up to speed, and general lost productivity. Since we started, 2020 aside, our annual staff turnover has been under 3 per cent. Nobody has left us for a direct competitor. That is our single proudest KPI. It's saved us a fortune, and we get to keep great staff.

So branding isn't some arts and crafts project compared to the real work of operations and finance. It's a vital business discipline that generates the margins that pay everyone's wages, including the brand sceptics who set the budgets.

Your brand won't work unless everyone in your business is on board. If marketing is only seen as a department, you don't have a brand. You just have a handful of your staff believing in the gleaming brand vision: the people who wrote it. Everyone else is just, 'Yeah, whatever.'

Don't underestimate the knowledge of your salespeople. There's traditionally been friction between marketing and salespeople. Marketers tend to regard sales and service people with mild contempt – for their lack of a degree, their embroidered shirts and their vulgar urge to design their own email footers in Comic Sans. Underestimating salespeople is a major mistake, because people who sell things all day soak up a lot of instinctive knowledge about people and what makes them buy. Good salespeople have near-psychic skills.

I've spent a lot of time lurking in stores with salespeople, watching them sell product I was writing ads for. The experienced reps would watch customers arrive and predict exactly what the customer would be looking for, what they would say, and whether they would buy or not. All before the customer had said a word. They were usually right. The experienced ones just read the non-verbal signals, tuned in by years of winning and losing sales.

They don't need to do customer satisfaction surveys on your products, because disgruntled customers have complained that information directly to their faces. Reps get to see products stress-tested in ways you can't imagine, by the sort of customers who have trouble with shoelaces. And they keep smiling.

Good frontline people are the essence of all that's positive about a brand. In most businesses, customers get more involved with your sales and service people than they do with any ad or website. And those sales and service people, on average, think the marketing people are out-of-touch wankers.

Salespeople know about accountability. Marketing people can get away with projects that deliver zero measurable return, because it created an intangible boost in 'brand equity'. That may be true, and a legitimate step on the pathway to profits, but see how a rep would go justifying a month without sales as 'building relationship equity'.

Getting everyone singing from the same page about your brand is a minor miracle. But it's so worth doing. When I was developing brands, we would spend half our time working with sales reps, engineers, project managers and so forth, trying to find a brand position they'd feel comfortable saying out loud. If it's not comfortable, they won't say it. Ever.

Brands that your whole staff don't get behind are like fridge magnets: a thin layer of colour and amusement that doesn't change what's beneath. If your brand message rings true for the majority of your staff, chances are it will resonate with clients. It probably answers a genuine issue. That means the business owner believes in it too, and means it when talking to staff. In the long run, that belief creates the company-wide momentum you need to achieve greatness.

CHARGE MORE
OR PERISH

'm not saying you should be a greedy monocled business person in a top hat, but you should always be thinking about how to charge more. There is constant relentless pressure to drop your prices: digital disruption, bottom-feeder procurement departments, new competitors willing to work for food. But your staff aren't coming to you looking for a pay reduction. Your landlord hasn't built in an annual rent decrease. If you're not constantly thinking about how to move your prices up, you're going backwards.

Look closely at who's doing your quoting, if you're not a published-price business. That's where your money is made or lost. After that, it's just execution, and you can't change much. If someone too weak or too nice does the quotes, their discounting will strangle your business. They'll think a 10 per cent discount means you make 10 per cent less profit. Depending on your margins, it might be 50 per cent less, or worse. So you have to do twice as much work as you would without the deal. So many effort-addicted business owners just knuckle down and accept this madness.

Every industry has its pricing orthodoxies. Look to other industries for inspiration. Why do people expect your product to be the same price everywhere, all the time? Try asking an airline or a hotel to match their low-season price all year. They are scientists at matching pricing to demand. How can you do it?

Consider the hell-category that is camera retailing. It's always been a price battleground, where customers spent days comparison shopping, even before smartphones ate the camera industry's lunch. Now it's mass murder for margins, with eBay full of international vendors with fake local presence pushing margins close to zero. Some retailers charge for a consultation with a salesperson, refundable if you buy a camera.

Yet fifteen minutes away, the international airport is a mega-mall of people buying cameras, watches and electronic junk like it was the Last Store On Earth, for prices well above what you'd pay downtown. It's pure herd memory. Because once upon a time, in about 1982 when cameras and gadgets were cheaper 'overseas', airport duty-free shops gave you tax-free deals without you having to negotiate with shady foreigners. Tax laws have changed and there are no bargains now. But people are in a holiday state of mind. They're excited, but bored because they had to check in two hours early. In the same way humpback whales make no logical decision to swim north in winter – they just do it – international travellers *know* they want a new watch or camera. Go on, treat yourself, they think.

How can you put clients under a similar spell that makes them pay over the odds for no good reason? Analyse your customers. Airlines don't just adjust their prices through low- and high-demand periods, they charge rich customers four times as much to avoid sitting near poor customers. How can you get more out of people who have more?

How soon do your customers want stuff? Can you charge more to those in a hurry? Consider risk, which people hate. How can you make your product feel like a safer choice than your competitors'? (Particularly if there are children or pets involved.)

There's a lot to play with. Understand the role of price as a quality signifier. If you had to choose one way to determine quality, it's price. High price equals high quality. Can you sell fewer, more expensive things?

T2 took an everyday product and applied a genius pricing strategy that would have got a respectful nod from Pablo Escobar.

Premium-brand English Breakfast tea in Woolworths: $17 a kilo. At T2, it's $120. T2 customers flock to their lovely stores and snap up their elegantly packaged gear. Supermarket tea will never make a thoughtful gift. Think how much less work you have to do when you're charging six times as much. How much you save on freight, rent, transaction costs and everything else. Yes, their marketing and packaging costs more, but not six times more.

High price can be pure perception. When you shop for a TV, there's always a super-expensive one on display that never gets sold. The sales-people talk it up, but they know you'll say, 'I love it, but I think I'll get the next model down.' You're still buying an expensive TV but it feels like great value because they changed your frame of reference. It's the opposite of the cheapest bottle on the restaurant wine list, which you will never buy for fear of your date or client seeing the real cheapskate you.

When you're starting out and you have nothing else to get your foot in the door, price deals are okay. If you genuinely believe that your service is better, it's a good way to get people to experience it the first time. It's a classic error to offer the discount but deliver in a shabby bargain-bin way, where your people give it less effort than they would for a full-price customer. Do a great job, and you'll probably win the customer. But then you'll have to be working relentlessly to drag your price up from this bargain baseline. If you're selling one product, it's tricky, but look at how you can add accessories, premium delivery, insurance or other conveniences people might pay for. It's a fine line between these and the slap-in-the-face ticket surcharge scams we'll look at later, but it's okay to cover legitimate costs.

Put prices up in small amounts more often. It seems obvious, but so many people only visit this issue every two years with a savage hike that makes corporate clients go out to tender again. Don't startle them. Treat it like a hostage situation. No sudden movements, only gradual change.

You will deal with all sorts of price-hustler clients. Like people who talk up how much potential business they have in store for you. In our business we get plenty of this. 'I do this sort of thing ten times a year. If you do this one for half-price, I'll use you exclusively for all the rest.'

No you won't, you lying ferret. Nobody who says this ever has more work beyond the bit they want a cheap deal on. I always say: 'That's great, book in all ten and we'll do the final one totally free.' They never do, and that's fine.

With business clients, the best way to understand pricing is to understand their commercial goals. In our business, new clients usually tell us they can get a better deal on technical equipment. If their event is a staff training day, the better deal might be fine. But if their CEO is on stage, what are the risks, and the cost when things go wrong? What grief will descend if the CEO's presentation fails? Most industry sales reps would say we're in the technology business. The smarter ones know we're in the CEO pain-minimisation business. That comes at a higher price, and it's worth it.

GO FOR
SILVER!

Look for brand positioning ideas that have worked for others in different fields. We looked to the original Mad Man, Bill Bernbach of Doyle Dane Bernbach (DDB), a trailblazing genius. Before Bernbach, American advertising was the worst kind of grandiose boasting: 'Cruise in the ultimate luxurious splendour in the all-new Crown Ambassador Sedan, with new Plush-o-Matic silky smooth suspension that won't upset your wife's hairstyle.'

Bernbach was the first to do advertising that spoke to you like your realistic friend. His early 1960s ads for the VW Beetle must have seemed, at the time, like they were written by aliens. A small picture of the car on a white background, with the headline 'Lemon'. And copy like: 'It's ugly, but it gets you there'. Those VW ads are still revered today, as trailblazing masterpieces of simple humanity. Apple borrowed a lot from them.

While Bernbach rose to fame, car-hire firm Avis was getting smashed by rival Hertz. Stumped, the Avis CEO called Bernbach and asked if he could sprinkle a bit of the old DDB magic on their brand. Unfortunately, his budget was modest. Could Bernbach help them out? Bernbach considered it. The biggest cost for any agency is the hourly expense of its people. Client middle management like to burn that time with long

119

meetings and whimsical changes to every ad. Bernbach offered to work to the Avis budget, but on the condition Avis had to accept DDB's ideas without meddling. To his credit, the Avis boss agreed.

DDB came up with the devastatingly effective 'When you're only No.2, you try harder'[4] campaign. The ads explained why Avis couldn't take you, the customer, for granted. They had to try harder because if you're not number one you can't rest on your laurels. It was genius. Every market has a number one and part of the target market always resents it. 'We Try Harder' launched in 1963. Like the VW work, it jumped out from the rest of the market for its refreshing modesty. Probably because it was written by a woman, Paula Green, who wanted to create an antidote to the boastfulness of the era. She would have known quite a bit about having to try harder, given the office culture of that era. 'Avis can't afford not to be nice.' 'Avis can't afford to make you wait.' 'Avis can't afford dirty ashtrays.'

Within a year, Avis went from losing $3.2 million to earning $1.2 million, its first profit in over a decade. Within a few years they had to drop the number two message because they were . . . number one. They continued with 'We Try Harder'. The campaign ran for fifty years. That is one solid gold positioning statement.

There was one ad we particularly liked. The headline was 'No.2ism: The Avis Manifesto'. With a hammer and sickle made from a tyre jack and mechanic's hammer, a gutsy image for an American ad in a time when folk lived under the shadow of Soviet nukes. It laid down the Avis doctrine:

The No.1 attitude is: 'Don't do the wrong thing. Don't make mistakes and you'll be OK.'

The No.2 attitude is: 'Do the right thing. Look for new ways. Try harder.'

It finished up with this invitation: 'Avis didn't invent No.2ism. Anyone is free to use it. No.2's of the world, arise!'

Anyone is free to use it. We were up against a much bigger competitor. That ad was all the invitation we needed. Business creativity is often just taking an existing idea and adapting it into a different industry. We took Avis up on their fifty-year-old offer. A proud number two we

120

would be. One slight issue: at the time we were something like number twelve by sales turnover. But who said you had to be number two in sales turnover? Sure, you could imply that. But it could be attitude. Or profitability. We ran with it.

We photographed all our staff doing the universal number two sign, with its historical reminder of Winston Churchill's World War II 'V for Victory' gesture. Our website preached the number two gospel. You have to try harder. Price better. Have better equipment. You can't take customers for granted. When the phone rings, you're excited. Our ads featured an Olympic podium with audiovisual technicians, the silver medal winner jumping like an excited madman while the gold guy just stood there.

Marketing aside, it gave our staff a blueprint for behaviour. There's a lot of meaning in the number two position. It was a constant compass pointing them in the right direction. We didn't have to keep telling them to try harder or be more enthusiastic. The best part was clients saying: 'You guys are so refreshingly modest, admitting to being number two and yet being so proud of it.'

Repeating short phrases about a million times can be tiring, but it works. You get sick of your own message long before your target market does. Five years later, when we retired the number two message, we had become that number two brand. Say it often enough and it comes true.

The task is to keep it consistent. Most businesses have a new marketing boss every two years, keen to put their personal stamp on the brand. They change the advertising, the positioning and their agencies. This creates a brand with multiple personality disorder. Multiple personalities make people nervous. Customers don't know what to expect, so they go elsewhere. If Avis can stick to a positioning for fifty years, you can commit to at least five.

FOR ALL YOUR
MARKETING NEEDS

Marketing is a Wizard of Oz act. We all try to make our business seem larger than it is, hoping nobody will discover the tiny old man working the cogs behind the curtain. You might be a one-person business running everything from cafés and libraries. But when the client sees your ad, website or sales pitch, they don't know how big your office is or how many staff you have. They just judge how it feels. We live in a golden era of virtual bluffing that can make your fledgling business look like a global powerhouse.

Unfortunately, businesses can signal their smallness with cheeseball pitch lines they think are top-shelf dealbait but in reality make them look one step up from a mobile dog wash. Let's look at a few common offenders.

Our team has a combined 85 years of industry experience

What does this even mean? One person with 45 years' experience who should have left the business years ago, and 20 others with two years' each? Year-totalling presents a dusty and confusing image of your team's skills.

Acme Services Pty Ltd

Small businesses love to add 'Pty Ltd' as if being a registered company is a badge of prestige and proof that you've hit the big time. Only your accountant cares.

Simply the best!

Anyone who does Australian highway drives knows there are only two kinds of pie shop: 'Australia's Best' and 'World-Renowned'. Hands-on pie experience has taught you that these claims sit somewhere between wild exaggeration and flagrant lie. People who *are* the best never say so, except Muhammad Ali, and none of us is Ali. Variations on this theme include 'You've tried the rest, now try the best!' but 'Simply the Best!' gets the Grand Swiss Cheeseball Award for evoking the 1980s motivational anthem. Say it and the client won't hear the rest of your message, because it's drowned out by the grating sax solo you planted in their mind.

For all your lawn care needs

Renting a holiday house is a fun trip back to ye olde marketing days. The internet doesn't work, so you must choose regional TV or a selection of DVDs from the *Four Weddings and a Funeral* era. Regional TV ads are all made in-house by the local channel using one overworked writer/director/cameraman named Damo. Damo doesn't have much spare time, so his ads fit a strict template. It must open on a shot of a van pulling up in front of a local business in an industrial estate. And it must end with 'For all your fabric needs!' or 'For all your birdseed needs!' or whatever. Try to break the Damo template.

Exclamation marks!!!

You might have noticed a theme throughout our small business claims so far: the exclamation mark. Nothing makes you look more like a small yappy Pekingese among the big dogs of business. Desperate for attention! Hey, look at me!! OMG they're multiplying like viruses!!! And if you want to create a clear impression that you are a thirteen-year-old girl, keep using them!!!!

Graphic clutter and giant logos

The old saying 'Nature abhors a vacuum' is never truer than in small business marketing. Small-business people can't stand blank space, because they want maximum value for their money. So they enlarge their logo to fill all the available space, creating a cramped, try-hard look. Elegance and assurance come from giving graphics room to breathe.

Then there are clichés beloved of hack marketers in businesses of all sizes.

Our people are our greatest asset

From the same mindset as 'It's our quality *and* our service'.

At Largecorp, we . . .

Opening with your name in your ad, proposal or whatever is a charmless habit. It's the 'But enough about me, tell me what you think about me' school of marketing. Does it get the customer's attention? No. Is there something exciting in it for them? No, it's just you saying your name again and again. For bonus cliché points, use: 'At Largecorp, we're *passionate* about . . .'

124

More than just (the thing you do)

Brands who say this usually do exactly the same as all their competitors, and no more. It's like the 'infinity plus one' line small boys use. A personal favourite: the recently departed naan brand 'Not Just Naans.' It was true, in the sense that you also got a plastic sleeve package, but apart from that: literally just naan. A close relative is 'Experience The Difference'. You can take this lazy claim as a guarantee there will be no difference.

Puns

There's a popular belief that marketing should get people's attention via jokes. This is not true. Marketing messages should show how your product alone can solve their problems, in as few words as possible. If humour works to do that, go for it, but it's harder than it looks. Being funny is hard for pro comedians who've refined their craft for decades on cruel, indifferent audiences. It's almost impossible for the fledgling business operator. Yet some dark instinct draws them to the cheapest humour tool of all: the pun.

To pick a random example I saw: bus stop ads for an international sandwich store brand promoting their coffee. Over a shot of a standard takeaway coffee sitting in a pile of beans, the headline: 'The Coffee everyone's BEAN talking about'. The ad is basically Dad reading out a Christmas cracker joke. Using capitals for 'BEAN' just makes it worse. You can practically hear a cartoon 'boing' sound effect. It's not clever, it's not funny and it's not selling your coffee.

There is a time and a place for puns in marketing: never and nowhere.

Study big brands that are already successful, and adapt their style. Just *having* a style puts you ahead of most. And enforce it: brands are built on years of visual consistency.

Old-school though it is, have a landline number and an actual office address. Sure, the landline will divert to your mobile and the office is a serviced one you never visit, but it shows substance. Without these details, clients sense you're a sole trader who may disappear at the first sign of trouble.

You can't do it on your own. Hire business writers and graphic designers. The collapse of paid media has left the market awash with great writers and designers who are remarkably affordable. They're heaps cheaper than accountants, and all accountants can do is say, 'Your revenues are too low', while communications professionals can help fix that situation.

THE OPPOSITE OF
MARKETING: BE HONEST

Marketing is hard, because other companies say they're perfect for everything. It's just white noise. So being honest is a radical standout move.

There is strength in saying 'We don't do that.' It makes your specialty claims more believable. There's so much One-Stop-Shop Syndrome out there, businesses claiming to cover all your needs, but they're mediocre at most of them. So a package print company adds a terrible creative department so they can offer 'total communication solutions'. Or a bathroom warehouse offers to do your bathroom design, to sell more taps and sinks. They put a D-team on the job and you're disappointed with the results.

As a creative director, I stopped doing radio campaigns, because the same thing happened every time. I'd plan a campaign using a range of media. I'd meet the radio station sales rep to book the spots. I made ads that would feel consistent across radio, TV, print and digital. But I forgot radio station sales reps are treacherous vermin.

After *every* campaign, they would call my client directly. 'You don't need to spend extra money on that wanker creative agency. We're a one-stop shop! We'll write and produce the ads in-house at no cost, so you only pay for the airtime!'

I could write a whole chapter on the horror of ads made by radio station in-house writers, who have to crank out thirty ads a day, so they use the same hack formulas over and over. Like where the voiceover guy stops reading halfway through the script and runs off to get his hands on those crazy bargains. To your radio station sales rep, that is some serious brand-building comedy gold. When you're high on your own one-stop shop fumes, you lose track of the fact that your product is garbage and you are screwing the person who actually brought you the business.

Admit to your weaknesses, and your strengths seem bigger. You don't have to pretend to be perfect, the way most brands do. Nobody really likes a perfect person. Flaws are interesting and sometimes endearing. My domestic appliance maker client called me to a planning meeting for their Mother's Day campaign. You can picture their proposed ads, because every Mother's Day ad looks the same. Ideal white couple sits on a couch with adorable kids, a boy and a girl, on the floor. Mum has a beatific smile because she's unwrapping the client's product. And the headline, the same since Mother's Day was invented: 'Spoil Mum This Mother's Day'.

Sigh. Really? I'm not a mum, but it's not a breakthrough insight to suggest that Mum probably doesn't want a kitchen appliance or any other tool of domestic slavery for Mother's Day. Unless 'spoil' is in the sense of 'Getting a rechargeable vacuum cleaner spoilt my entire fucking Mother's Day.'

So I suggested that it was time the company confessed their sins after decades of self-centred and downright wrong Mother's Day gifts. We proposed a website called No More Toasters, dedicated to stamping out gift ideas that effectively say: Mum, here's something you can use to do more work for the rest of us. It also advised Dad and the kids on what appliances Mum might actually like. An espresso maker, for example. Or a cocktail blender.

There were other handy tips, like how to buy flowers for Mum. 'Anything with baby's breath says: we bought this at the servo on the way home.' There was a formal apology from the company for all the gifts of irons, kettles and vacuum cleaners over the years.

This was confronting for the client. The belief that all your products are awesome all the time dies hard. It took about twenty meetings, but bless them, they approved it. We ran it with an ad and PR campaign, encouraging mums to call radio stations with tales of their worst-ever Mother's Day gifts.

The centrepiece of the website was the Hall of Shame, where mums could post their shocking gifts. Oh my God, it touched a nerve. There were outpourings from mums all over the country sharing Mother's Day horrors. Pictures flooded in. Sheds. Alloy car wheels. Mismatched bargain-bin lingerie. Pole dancing lessons. CB radios. A washing machine with only the first payment made, so Mum had to pay the rest off over two years. My favourite was from a gay guy: 'I bought Mum two tickets to *The Lion King*, but accidentally put in my two tickets to a leather dance party. Couldn't work out why she wasn't excited.'

And even though the client was theoretically apologising for decades of gift crimes, the overall customer response was: thank you so much for finally owning up to it. The campaign won national awards for sales effectiveness. Refreshingly honest confessions had sold far more appliances than the standard schmaltz. And made that brand feel a lot more real in the process.

Put yourself in the shoes of the customer. Talk honestly to them about the good and the bad. In our industry, nobody ever says no. They keep taking bookings right up until the last minute, because work is work. We hate saying no, because it hurts, but sometimes we have to draw the line. You'll get a call from a new client you've been chasing for years: they've finally got some business for you. But it's on the same day as lots of other big projects.

Sometimes we've had to be honest and say: 'Sorry, we could take it on, but all the good people and equipment are already booked out with existing clients and if we said yes to this, you would get the B- or C-team of freelancers. Which would create completely the wrong impression on your first event. Sorry, but we'll have to pass.'

Every time they've said how impressed they were at this honesty, because everyone else says yes and doesn't warn them of the risks involved. It's usually led to more work later, because you get a reputation for straight talk.

ADMIT YOU DON'T KNOW

I'm always troubled by the perception of salespeople being liars, because many customers are massive liars themselves. Spend some time on a returns desk and you'll hear tales that would embarrass Donald Trump. Being in business means dealing with supplier salespeople, and that's an experience that ranges between inspirational and homicidal. The good ones ask questions. The bad ones talk like one of those string-pull dolls with six catchphrases. *Pulls string* 'The perfect end-to-end solution!'

How do you know which ones will let you down? Listen. The words people use give away so much. I'm lucky enough to work in an industry where most salespeople are pretty ethical. But I've had some interesting debates about the porkiest lies salespeople use, the words that light up your brain's lie detectors like an aerial night shot of New York. Every instinct tells you that green-lighting this purchase carries the level of misplaced optimism you see in anyone marrying an actor or musician.

There were some strong Top Lie contenders. 'Turnkey solutions.' 'Thought leaders.' '110 per cent.' You've heard each of these claims coming out of a confident tosser who then lets you down in a blink. But as a sign that you're dealing with a straight-up, forked-tongue bullshit artist, the prize goes to people who say 'seamless'. Everything in life has seams. Salespeople who promise 'seamless' don't know how to deliver it. Like a performing animal, they've been trained that if they say the magic word someone might give them some money. But it's not very persuasive, because words are easy to say, and there's an infinite supply of other people who also say them.

It's fascinating observing the differences between what people say and what they do. And what they *are*. People who actually are cool never describe themselves or their businesses as cool. Honest people rarely say 'Trust me'. Then there's *relationship*. Did you ever start a meaningful relationship with anyone by saying: 'I'd like to have a relationship with you'? No, because that would be a strange, stalker thing to say. I have dozens of business cards from Relationship Managers at bank branches. 'Relationship Manager' is the language of people with no idea that relationships come from what you do, not what you say you're going to do. And they have always been transferred to another branch by the next time I've needed something.

For some reason, marketing people who say 'savvy' are in the least competent quartile of that profession. If you hear the word 'guru', reach for your pistol. You will get really pedestrian creative work from anyone who uses the words 'quirky', 'pizzazz' or 'wow factor'. I once had a client send back a TV script asking for more of the first two, but spelt 'qwerky', like their cat had walked across the keyboard.

A rule of creative people is that the really good ones never use the word 'creative' about themselves. They're too busy doing the hard work of producing excellent creative things. The less skilled the creative, the more undergraduate affectations are on display: the scarves, the Penguin Classics iPad cover, the Pantone coffee mug, and the general vibe that you, the client, will never understand the existential pain of true creative genius. Thanks, Jean-Paul Sartre, but no budget for you.

Then there are the words your salespeople use internally. If 'apples' come up, you're not dealing with a sales champion. When crap salespeople lose the sale, they're convinced the competitor tricked the customer into buying the wrong product for a lower price.

'I said to them, you're not comparing apples for apples.'

This is the mindset of an apple grower, who loves apples more than anything, and is convinced apples are the answer to any customer need.

131

Maybe the client is perfectly happy not to have an apple. Send your product-obsessed sales rep to fruit-deprogramming camp to widen their grasp of client benefits, or they will keep losing sales with their relentless apple focus.

You know who I like to work with? People who are comfortable saying 'I don't know'. Because so many people feel they should have something to say on every topic. And when they don't have objective knowledge or experience, they like to reckon things. This is how many new business ideas get 'researched'.

'We actually found it didn't get a very good response with the people we tested it on.'

'Okay. Was that by any chance your receptionist? Or your brother-in-law?'

'Uh . . . yes. But they know quite a bit about what they like.'

These people have the all-important Bachelor of What I Reckon from the University of Life. If you ask them something, they're going to feel they should have an opinion on it, no matter how half-arsed. It's also an issue with egotist managers. So many problems stem from senior execs who believe they will lose prestige unless they hand down God-like expertise in every situation.

I have so much respect for people who say: 'I don't know enough about that topic to comment. Ask someone who does.' And for managers who say: 'That's not my strong area, what do you think we should do?' Confidence is important in leadership, but it doesn't mean talking up how great you are at every opportunity. There is greater strength in sometimes admitting you don't know, and seeking guidance.

In general, talking things up too much is counterproductive. Consider the life cycle of a business project. An exciting idea. Energetic planning. Assembling teams. Rolling out the product. It gets there, but it never quite goes as well as everyone wanted. It's rare for a new product or initiative to go better than you hoped. But getting to, say, 70 per cent of your target is probably a great result for all the work.

So the art of business is minimising how much you fail to meet your hopes and dreams. The reason things fail to meet those hopes and dreams is because staff and suppliers were talking up how 'seamless' and 'guaranteed' things were. Goals and expectations get inflated to wild fantasy. I'd rather work with people who say: 'We're going to do a good job and try our hardest.' People who talk realistically usually deliver real results. This is why salespeople who have hands-on experience in product delivery can be very successful, because they're less prone to uninformed 'reckonings', and customers can tell.

In our business, we make much better margins using salespeople who are basically show technicians, who tell it to people straight and don't say yes to everything. Not in a negative, roadblock sense, but in a practical, positive way: selling designs that work instead of pushing shiny things that won't. Saying yes to everything puts stress on your delivery systems, gives people unrealistic expectations, and sets up the fail.

FORGET THE
BIG SCORE

Everyone dreams their business will take off like the podcast success stories. They launch a marketing campaign then wait for the storm of incoming sales, and the Big Deal that catapults them to the easy life. Like the teeth-whitening duo who skyrocketed to multi-millionairedom off a Kylie Jenner post. Good on those guys, but it's a rarity. And that's okay. It's the basics that will get you there. Success is more of a gradual, tidal change you hardly notice as it builds.

Consistency is essential. Particularly in service industries, where it takes ages for people to get to know you. You'll easily spend three goldfish years patiently repeating the same message to people you've pitched to before. They promise to try you next time, then immediately forget you exist.

Through all this, you have to keep the marketing exposure frequent and the message consistent. Back when print was big, I used to get marketing clients calling me on a Thursday afternoon, because they had scored an amazing last-minute deal on a full page in the weekend paper. Another ad had dropped out, so they got it for $10,000 instead of $30,000. Could we get ad art ready in two hours? They viewed it as an atom bomb solution, a monster blast of exposure to catapult their sales to the next level. And the customer response would be: pretty much nothing.

It doesn't work that way, analog or digital. Most people aren't thinking about buying your product on that one day you run your blockbuster campaign. So it's not on their radar. You're much better running small but consistent ads long term. Abandon your dream to 'go viral'. That was every client brief when online video first appeared. Going viral is not a thing you choose to do. It's a random lightning strike of luck that can't be wished or marketing-briefed into reality any more than a sixteen-year-old boy's hopes of being picked up by a supermodel can.

Let's imagine you did suddenly get 30 million views of your video worldwide. One of two things will happen. The most likely thing is: not much, sales-wise, because a mega-viewed video doesn't always translate into a reason to buy your product. Plus most viewers will be in places your product doesn't exist. If it *does* give you a monster surge in sales, unless your product is a download, chances are you won't have the stock, staff or systems to deal with it. So your customers will get a broken experience. Then the decision: do you gear up to deal with the surge, knowing it's probably a one-off? That would be a mad risk. It's not exactly the stuff that business dreams are made of.

There's so much expectation attached to marketing campaigns. I always enjoy hearing people talk of sending an 'e-blast'. All that rocket thrust imagery for something that will pass unnoticed on its way to a lonely spambox grave. You're always better off to go tortoise rather than hare. I've observed this ancient behaviour model literally as a tortoise owner. My beloved childhood tortoise Albert passed away recently. They can move surprisingly fast, and they always go in the same direction. I'll spare you a whole chapter of tortoise–business metaphors. Let's just say modest but continuous marketing will help grow your business at a speed you can cope with.

I'm sceptical of people who talk about the Big Score, the massive sale that will transform everything, like movie criminal chat. 'It'll pay off my entire mortgage', 'It's in the bag – just one more manager needs to sign off, but that's a formality'. A few months later, you ask how it went and they relate the unlucky turn of events that killed the deal just before the order got processed. I'm really superstitious about telling people of a big prospective deal. Putting it out there just increases the odds of the wheels falling off, adding embarrassment to your disappointment.

You'll win the odd big client on your business journey, and it's a lovely feeling, but it shouldn't be your only pursuit. Get lots of smaller ones, and then gradually you start to accumulate larger ones. This kind of big-win urge also leads to stalled marketing programs. Major initiatives sit on the tarmac for months awaiting permission to launch, because everyone's waiting for every detail to be perfect. Meanwhile, they're doing nothing. You're much better rolling out something smaller now, even if it's a bit dirty.

I'm not going to do specific campaign advice because the book will be out of date in ten minutes, but here's an overall tip: get an outsourced expert to run your digital media. Trying to stay on top of the latest updates and mood changes of Facebook, Instagram, Google and the rest is like trying to get a large octopus into a small bucket. Those algorithms are so squirmy. You get one bit under control and another has completely changed direction. Their back-end controls are a hellscape of ever-changing options. Keeping up is a full-time job you don't have time to do. Most platforms offer simplified campaigns you can set up yourself. They are basically vacuum cleaners that suck the money out of your account and deliver little. Ask other business owners if they can recommend a digital agency or freelancer.

THE $15,000 COFFEE AND OTHER WAYS TO REPEL CUSTOMERS

The customer experience is one of the few ways left to stand out now. It pains me as an ex-creative director that marketing has never looked as generic as it does now. Every SME website is a standard template full of stock photos, and they all look the same. Every shitty pop-up ad looks the same. Facebook and Instagram even more so. They're purpose-built to ensure every brand feels identical. No competitive advantage means an endless click-price auction and only Mark Zuckerberg wins.

So when a customer gets in touch, that's your big chance to stand out and make that customer a fan. Their first purchase is your audition for a happy future together. Most of us come to work each day with the intention of doing a good job and not pissing our clients off. Yet sometimes we do things to make customers think: *You started out* so good *and now you are deeply disappointing. What happened?* It often begins when all your meetings focus on internal processes.

Urged on by your finance people, you start believing your customers understand those processes and don't mind the inconvenience they bring. Plus finance have some exciting new ideas on how to boost the ol' P&L. That's where the trouble starts.

I used to use an audio studio for radio ads and soundtracks. They did quality work, and were pleasant to deal with. I would spend about a thousand dollars a job with them, maybe fifteen times a year. I turned up one January morning for a session. The studio manager appeared.

'Morning, Ian, we're getting coffee. Do you want one?'

'Sure, thanks.'

A week later I got their invoice.

Four hours of studio time, $880. Coffee, $3.80.

I called up, assuming it was a mistake.

'Uh . . . what's with charging me for the coffee?'

She switched to Adminsplaining Mode, where people snap from their normal personality into schoolteacher tone and rhythm. The first word out of their mouth is always 'Well . . .'

'Well, we all had a Strategy Day for our business going forward. Our feedback was that our customers wanted the lowest hourly rate possible, with any extras charged on an as-used basis. We felt customers would understand that costs have to be recouped.'

Tip: *recoup* is not a word your clients want to hear. There is no good context for *recoup*. Also, 'Our customers want us to be cheaper.' Duh. If you ask them, what do you think they'll say?

'Okay, but you didn't tell me any of that. You just offered it and became the first non-café business in my entire career to charge me for a coffee.'

'Oh. Well, none of the other customers have queried it.'

I never used them again. It felt so . . . dirty. An offer of a coffee is the most basic transaction unit of human hospitality. It was like being billed for a handshake or business card. That's $3.80 'recouped'. Fifteen-thousand odd dollars of revenue per year lost. Not a great ratio. Put that on a Post-It note at your next Strategy Day.

Moves like this are like a magician's, but in a bad way. Magicians distract you with a *Hey, look over there!* move while they do their sneaky work to set up the entertainment.

Coffee on the invoice shouts HEY, CHECK THIS OUT! Sure, we did $880 worth of perfectly good work, but ignore that! Here's an UNJUS-TIFIED CHARGE THAT WILL ANNOY YOU A THOUSAND TIMES MORE THAN THE DOLLAR AMOUNT INVOLVED.

Invoice items are such a fertile field for customer annoyance, because it's the customer's last memory of the whole experience. Customers don't really understand the price of what you do, but everyone understands a coffee. If you're, say, a lawyer, your hourly rate is a mystical synthesis of your skills, experience and reputation. But everyone knows the price of a photocopy. If you choose obvious everyday items to maximise your job profit, they'll assume everything else you do is marked up to the same extortionate level. It makes a great story that people can tell over and over again, with your brand as the villain.

Then there's screwing customers right at the end of their purchase experience just because you can. You buy movie tickets, which are already expensive. You click to agree to their posted price. Then the last thing you remember is being charged an *extra* $3 'transaction' fee. *Per fucking ticket*, for the sweet privilege of . . . spending money with them. Like their computer server has to do four times more work than for a single ticket. Think I'll watch Netflix.

Let's be clear: there is no 'admin fee', 'convenience fee', 'transaction fee' or any other name you want to give it that isn't a customer annoyance felony. It creates the perception that you had a deal, they agreed to it, and now you want *more*, just because.

Imagine if supermarkets, whose checkouts are a much higher capital investment than movie ticket websites, charged an extra 15 per cent levy just for paying for your groceries. There would be angry mobs. As with cabs and their decades of 10 per cent credit card surcharges, it's hard to feel sympathy when the disrupters come for industries that have been screwing us for years. I'll be lighting cigars while I watch them burn.

6.

PEOPLE

BUSINESS ISN'T AS COMPLEX AS THEY WANT YOU TO THINK

Here's a dark secret: lots of businesses have too much management. Management isn't the part of the business that makes the money. But damn, managers are good at creating that impression. So they can create empires for themselves and waste endless amounts of productive people's time via meetings and report writing.

Managers create that illusion through secret language. Here's how it works. You take a good question like 'Will people buy our product?' and translate it to 'What quantum of product-market fit is required across target verticals within total addressable market to resolve pain points and deliver a compelling value proposition?'

Present this with a vast spreadsheet nobody will ever check and a flow chart nobody understands, and now you're the only one who can do the job. It's no different to high priests in the Middle Ages, who rationed the secret information so the peasantry couldn't get above their station. Mysticism creates power. You can't understand what managers are talking about, so you assume they're smarter and better-educated than you. They should naturally be in charge.

That is not always the case. Workers on the front line are often better placed to understand what the company should do, and what its customers think. Because they have met some customers. Can I suggest an entire management theory in twelve words?

Better people on the front line – as few as possible in management.

Sure, it's short and understandable, so it won't cut much ice with the MBA crowd. It's also really profitable. Great frontline staff are the heart and soul of your organisation. They're the ones that generate the income and make your customers return.

Management in general is a self-multiplying system, creating more managers who go into battle with each other in a posturing and lobbying frenzy. Fascinating, if you're just watching it from a detached viewpoint like you're at the chimp enclosure. If you're paying for it, it's frustrating and heaps expensive.

Look at what happened during COVID-19. Overnight, people went from constant management supervision to working alone and it was generally . . . fine. They still got their work done. Sure, 100 per cent remote work isn't the future. But as a scientific experiment, it was clear evidence that people can get by with much less management than managers would like to think.

Management is different to leadership. You need leaders more than ever in these stressful times. Regular, non-managerial people can lift themselves to amazing heights if they feel they're recognised and are given the freedom and power to do their best. With a good leader, others step up and become leaders within their group. It becomes a virtuous cycle. My experience has been that there is zero correlation between leadership qualities and formal business qualifications.

When we started our business I wrote the Scene Change Ten Commandments, a quick summary written on a plane from gut instinct:

1. Look after the crew.
2. If it will make us money, buy it now.
3. Chase profitability, not size. We don't have to be everywhere.
4. We are comfortable saying no.
5. We're in this to create long-term income, not to float or sell off to finance pigs.
6. Low group overheads.

7. Talk to people rather than emailing everything.
8. One short report a month is fine.
9. Make the good people think: 'I want to work *there*.'
10. No fucking Blackberries.

If the answer wasn't in that list, stage two was: Do the opposite of whatever private equity would do.

All but one commandment is as relevant to us today as it was then. On the Blackberries point, we weren't to know the iPhone would appear later that year to bring us all 24-hour work contact. We'd come from an environment with the classic corporate Blackberries that pinged all evening with demands from head office, wanting immediate answers. We don't want that vibe in our business.

Did the commandments work? Yes, it delivered year-on-year growth so tidy that our graph would get a tick from Marie Kondo. It's been profitable enough to pay for all our capex growth plus generate consistent dividends.

You don't need massive processes to run most businesses. Because – news flash – people don't read instructions. As Elon Musk put it, 'Any product that needs a manual to work is broken.' The more your people can think for themselves, and the more you let them do it, the better your business.

PEOPLE DON'T CHANGE

An interesting part of clocking up a few decades of work – and life –
is seeing how much people you've known since you were oily teens
have changed. They haven't, at all. Their personality, energy, openness
to new ideas, ethic for getting things finished, and the way they treat
others all stay the same. Their priorities adjust as they go through different phases of career and family, but their essential nature is fixed.

They haven't really changed since childhood, and there's nothing
they can do about it, locked as everyone is into turning into their own
parents, no matter how hard they fight it. It becomes clear when you
start hosting kids' birthday parties. There's always one standout selfish
horror child. You match them up to the parents, and of course it's
the child of the entitled Marcus and Cassandra who parked everyone
in with their Range Rover and interfered in pass-the-parcel to help
their kid score the major prize. In two decades, that child will be
taking credit for other people's ideas at work, and demanding a
larger desk.

The idea that people can change radically is bogus. The idea that
you can change them is deluded. Many women will be familiar with
men saying: 'I can change.' The sort of man who says this is more likely
to solve global warming than change any part of his character. So stop

146

thinking you can change staff. We're not talking about skills here. You can usually teach those.

What you can't change is their essential nature. If they're liars, they'll keep lying. If they're lazy, they will be lazy until they die. There's no intervention you can stage on people's core character, no seminar you can send them to. It's like sending your rabbit to a course on not eating lettuce. It's a waste of their time and your money. Your instincts about staff after a few months are correct. Act on them. 'I'm giving you one more warning' never delivers.

Please feel free not to write to me about someone you know who genuinely did change. The world has many people, and it's theoretically possible. It's just really unlikely and your time is precious. Think of the time you've spent worrying about underperformers, coaching them on how to do better. Think how much of that effort ended up being productive in the end. Indeed.

There's also a persistent myth that you simply can't fire people. Sure you can. And if it costs you money, it's still the best investment you can make. Whatever it costs, having someone you don't want in your business is costing you far more in burnt clients and pissed-off co-workers. Consider the kind of team you want. You can't keep people who complain all day and consistently let their workmates down. It's a powerful statement to remove white-anters, who would survive for years in other businesses, because they're disrespecting the ethic of your A-team. Your other staff will thank you for it. As a bonus, your cast-offs will get jobs with your competitors. A double win and strategic masterstroke.

The flip side is that if you run across great people and you don't currently have a position available, consider hiring them and finding something for them to do. The role will evolve into something rewarding for both of you, because they can't change either. They can't stop being enthusiastic, innovative, energetic or whatever draws you to them. Whenever we do this, it's so much more worthwhile than recruiting from a pile of CVs. It's helped us grow the company much faster and, as a bonus, the snowball effect attracts more of those people.

It's great to be in business long enough to watch how people's characters build their careers long term. I'm a big fan of mentoring. Done well, it's so beneficial for both parties. But there's another type of mentoring I recommend as you navigate your career: negative mentoring. You haven't heard of it before because I made the name up, but here's how it works.

Observe people in meetings and at industry get-togethers. Talk to as many as you can. After a while, you'll get to know people who have never really amounted to much. They're getting on in years, and they're still account managers for a third-tier brand. They change jobs a lot. They will have gossip to share. They'll give you snarky asides about the real reasons someone else won that contract and how industry awards are rigged. You can sense their bitterness over opportunities lost and former workmates who have gone on to great things.

There's a line of thought that you should avoid those people, because successful people don't mix with negative types. This is shallow, childish thinking. Study these people, and discuss their work history and how they do things. You'll learn so much about what not to do and how not to think. Then, when you're tempted to make some snarky roadblock comment in a meeting, the spectres of your anti-role models urge you, 'Go for it! That's what we would do!' It's a sobering image to keep you on the path of righteousness.

Obviously, seek out the good people in the room as well. But if there aren't any free, soak up all the influences you can: weird, bad, whatever. It's all good experience and you'll develop a sixth sense for the anti-mentor, so you can avoid employing their kind.

I owe a lot to negative mentoring. When I set up my marketing agency, I'd go to client meetings with other agencies and consultants. That was where I first ran into the Grey Ponytail, a sobering vision of my future unless I took action. The Grey Ponytail isn't an individual: there are entire tribes of them, with the same look and same habits.

The Grey Ponytail used to work for a big jingle-based ad agency in the 1980s. On the gentle downhill slope towards his final paying position, he became creative director at a lower-ranked outfit. His red nose was testament to years of going to the pub for lunch and staying there. He had the floral shirt to signify creativity, with a light dusting of dandruff from the rarely washed ponytail. His off-colour jokes, patronising explanations of production methods and rampant meeting-room manspreading horrified the young female brand managers. He had no time for the childish distractions of that passing fad, the internet.

He used that repellent line, 'Get the old creative juices flowing.' Whenever I hear it, I think: Mate, please, keep your old juices to yourself. He was the full Dickens *Christmas Carol* warning of what I could become unless I got my act together.

I realised marketing creatives aren't cute past a certain age. They're just sad and powerless. I was in my thirties. Did I want to hit forty-five, pitching to a room of clients twenty years younger, trying to convince them that my ideas were 'on point'? No, I fucking didn't. Even at this early stage of my agency business, I was thinking how to set up my own brand, where I could be the client and head off the threat of Grey Ponytailhood.

It took three years before I acted, but the time spent thinking through the details is important. By the time the scale of the problem becomes apparent, when the client says: 'Sorry, but your ideas are kinda out of date with today's buyers, so we're changing suppliers,' it's too late to start looking for the escape hatch.

So cheers to those Grey Ponytails for your unwitting anti-guidance. I hope you're out there enjoying 'a few frothies', and I'm pleased on your behalf that the Mambo shirt has made an ironic comeback with the kids. Your collection will be worth a fortune.

MORNING PEOPLE WOULD VERY MUCH LIKE YOU TO KNOW ABOUT IT

Anyone on LinkedIn will recognise the Morning Routine Flex. A tech or finance bro updates the world on how he starts each weekday. Mark, a 'Neural Network HR' man, says:[5]

5.30 am	Wake up, get dressed, walk to gym
5.45 am	Get to gym
6.45 am	Walk home from gym
7.00 am	Take a very hot shower and switch it to the coldest temperature halfway through for thirty seconds
7.20 am	Cook four egg whites and blend up a smoothie with vegan protein
7.45 am	Rotate between HeadSpace for meditation or commit to language learning on Duolinguo
8.05 am	Drink one litre of water
8.15 am	Head to office and start accomplishing my daily goals.

Comment [with] your favourite morning routine below. Looking forward to seeing how fellow LinkedIn superstars start their day.

Thanks, Mark. If I had all that time in the morning I'd use it to reflect on what these needy, approval-craving updates really say about you. And your 'fellow LinkedIn superstars'.

When you're a small child, grown-ups listen enthralled as you tell them what you just did. Part of being an adult is realising they're not actually interested, and they're just humouring you. 'Oh, you drank a *whole litre of water*? What a *clever boy*!' Morning routine announcements are like when people tell you about the interesting dream they had last night.

Others take the 4.30 am Challenge, introduced to the corporate world by an ex-Navy SEAL whose name alone makes me afraid: Jocko Willink. People photograph their clock at that wretched hour each morning and post it, like hostage proof-of-life. GIVE ME FIFTY PUSH-UPS, SOLDIER! Early starts have been success gospel forever. It stems from the Protestant work ethic. In the subconscious business mind, pleasure takes place at night-time: illicit, ungodly behaviour that will distract you into lowering your work output. Better bring those urges under control.

We all know the proverb: 'Early to bed, early to rise makes a man healthy, wealthy and wise'. It first appeared in John Clarke's *Paroemiologia Anglo-Latina* in 1639. Choice advice for the blacksmith or turnip cropper at a time when capitalism was just kicking off. Now, not so much. As more of every job gets eaten by software, one of the few commercial advantages is to have better ideas than other people. On average, the people who have interesting new ideas tend to work later hours than the status quo maintenance team. If you love routine so much that you post your morning list, remember: routine tasks are the easiest to replace with code.

I've tried all the daily success habits at one time or another. I want them all to work, and many do. I won't tell you details because they're boring, it's different for everyone, and there's already an infinite supply of advice. One plan that didn't work for me was 5 am starts. Three weeks of them, 'to create permanent behaviour change'. They made me feel ill. I felt like I had to unstick my tongue from the roof of my mouth with a teaspoon. I'd do the exercise, write the to-do lists, be at my desk at 6.30 am. It felt good to get some work out of the way, but that work was pedestrian, tick-a-box stuff. It *felt* like work. There were zero flashes of inspiration. I hated it a lot.

In normal life, from about 10 am on, I'm feeling the love of work. I like working at night. It's better than watching *The Block* and my brain

151

feels fully warmed up by then. None of my night comrades will ever let you know that we're **#crushingit #uplate #owlpower**. Because you don't care. And we don't feel we're better than morning people. It works for us, and each to their own working habits.

Morning people would very much like you to know that mornings are best. The earlier, the more prestigious. They never tire of telling you that you should try it; your life will never be the same. How much have they already achieved while you were still asleep? Don't worry, they'll be posting it. I'm happy that early works for them, but the belief that everyone is the same as you is a massive liability in business. It stops you understanding staff and customers. Telling people to be more like you is not persuasive or endearing.

The early cult ignores a couple of real-life factors. One: sleep. The science is increasingly in that sleep is really good for you. Which is nice, speaking as a big fan of sleeping. Without enough of it, all your dawn workouts and meditations may count for nothing in your overall productivity. Two: children. They are purpose-built to destroy your puny plans. Yes, it's good to be up before them to calibrate your brain before the madness. But if they've kept you up half the night, just get all the sleep you need to survive. If you have children, time management advice from people who don't is like getting chin-up tips from a tyrannosaurus.

I had to stop listening to a major podcast I really liked because it would always open with a quarter-hour about morning routines. Expressed as if they were the single most important factor in high achievement. And not just 'Hey, so how do you start the day?' Relentless drilling down into specific breakfast details like a food scientist.

'At 6.45 am every day, I have a single bowl of steel-cut oats with oat milk and six blueberries.'

Cue five minutes of earnest discussion about why steel-cut will make you more successful than regular oats. Now 10,000 pod disciples are clamouring for specific oat types like it's Popeye's spinach, when they should be thinking about bigger issues. Breakfast has a long history of made-up bullshit about its importance.

Your mother would have told you that breakfast is the most important meal of the day. My mum says it to this day. Who discovered this cornerstone of nutrition science? The World Health Organization? A team of metabolic researchers at Yale? No, it was entirely made up by copywriters at General Foods' ad agency in 1944 to get people to eat Grape Nuts breakfast cereal. Now it's unshakable folklore embedded in our primal brains for generations.

Genius and elite performance do not come from breakfast. Just lay off the Froot Loops. Winston Churchill drank two bottles of champagne every day between 1908 and 1965, and he got some leadership done. (Data courtesy of Pol Roger, his preferred champagne house, who logged all the invoices after his death.)

The success industry makes you look at essential areas of life through a microscope when they're better viewed with the naked eye from a few steps back. Want to know what sort of exercise you need to be successful? *Some* fucking exercise. It's not about whether you do a hyper-iso kettle routine with anaerobic carb detonation or a twenty minute jog with the dog. It's whether you do any exercise at all. Most start exercising hard, then work up to none. By all means, get right into it, but remember it's extremely hard to excel at both business *and* exercise. Pick your battles and be realistic about where your talents lie. You only have so much time.

Morning-person syndrome stems from the same place as the constant need to tell people how busy you are. Night people seem more relaxed and less worried about what others might think. Recently I co-interviewed consumer psychologist Rory Sutherland, vice-chair of ad agency Ogilvy. This affable Welshman is my business Jesus. His book *Alchemy* analyses the deep-down illogic of consumers, and pulls apart the pseudo-accurate predictions of the spreadsheet people who control business. If you don't read it, customers and people in general will remain a confounding mystery.

The call was booked in for 5 pm Sydney time, 9 am in Rory's rural home in the UK. Five pm came and went. No Rory. That's cool, he's a very busy chap, he'll be there soon. The producer called Rory's assistant. Nothing. At 6.09 pm, after setting the new world record for Zoom pre-meeting banter, we all agreed to pull the pin. As we reached for the Leave Meeting button, our quarry surfaced in the Zoom waiting room like Moby Dick.

'Really sorry,' said Rory. 'I woke up for the interview, but then I fell asleep again.'

I bow down to the poised strength of this Non-Morning Guy openness. If anyone could get away with an excuse like 'Sorry, the client CEO in Hong Kong wanted an urgent call', he could. A morning person would have made an excuse. Rory fired up the vape and launched straight into ninety-five minutes of fascinating insights without drawing breath. It was the exact opposite of every breakfast meeting I've ever been to.

Rory spoke of how the entire work world is designed around the preferences of extroverts. Offices are designed to put people in your face all day. Gatherings are set up for the needs of show-offs who want to work the room. Introverts just have to put up with it. But what of differing body clocks?

Now that we've done a full reset on all working habits and realised there is no need for people to be supervised every hour of the day, business and entire cities could benefit from a rethink of working hours.

A city bar and restaurant owner I know had a good suggestion. Two-shift office hours: one from 7 am to 3 pm, another from 9 am to 5 pm. Or even 11 am to 7 pm. Choose which suits you. Workers are happier to do hours that suit them. Traffic and public transport congestion: halved. CBD bars and restaurants don't have to staff up for one ninety-minute surge at lunchtime. They can do a couple of lunch sittings and a less peaky evening, and now they're a much more viable business. Those businesses need to survive for life to return to our cities.

Whatever your preferences, it's important to keep an open mind. Not everyone is right all the time. My annoyance at the 4.30 am Challenge posts led me to read one of Lieutenant-Commander Jocko's books. Yes, he looks like a man who will tear your head off. And like many high-end military people, he's much more thoughtful than the stereotype suggests. He had valuable stuff to teach me, and so do most people. Just borrow the ideas that work for you. Especially the ones in those books you get to read after your 5 am start friends are sound asleep.

THE ART OF
ADVICE FILTERING

One of our staff was expecting his first child. Summoning memories of that exciting time, I pulled him aside and said: 'Would you like some advice?'

'Uh . . . sure.'

I quite enjoyed seeing him try to stay polite while he was thinking: If someone gives me just one more bit of new-parenting advice I will sever their head, put it in the freezer and use it as a prop for the kid's first Halloween.

'You're about to swamped by advice on every baby topic imaginable. And almost all of it will be rubbish. Ignore most of it and you'll be fine. Sorry to tell you that via the medium of advice.'

He seemed relieved he didn't have to pretend to appreciate the tip. People love to give you advice, and those who most want to give it are the last people on earth you want it from. Some only give advice to those who actively seek it. That's likely to be good advice. You should ask accomplished people for their thoughts and they're usually delighted to provide them. It makes you smarter and makes them feel good.

The major source of advice, though, is from people who like to thrust it upon you. 'You know what you should do?' is their standard opening line after a minimal appraisal of your situation. The Advice

Thruster usually has poor listening skills, equipped as they are with all the knowledge anyone would ever need. They bring certainty that everyone else has exactly the same tastes, values and morals as they do. You won't find them asking about the individual details of your problem. They won't leave many gaps in the conversation even if you feel like clarifying anything. They won't notice your non-verbal lack of interest signals.

Their advice boils down to: 'You should be more like me. Because what I'd do is the best thing to do in any given situation.' Advice Thrusters are immune to professional advice from so-called experts because experts don't operate in the 'real world' and can be overruled by 'common sense'.

Your difficulties with other people are a particular favourite of the Advice Thruster. They're so confident of what they would do if they were you. Troubles with the boss? You should really tell her straight up where to stick her demanding requests. Kids being uncontrollable little bastards? I'd really come down much tougher on them; kids today have no discipline. Distant cousins from England overstaying their welcome in the house? Just tell them they have to be out in two days and if they're not gone, you're going to put their luggage out in the street.

There is no limit to the tough justice they're willing to let you hand out in difficult situations to people they don't know. I sometimes invite them to the meeting where they've advised a Putinesque shirtfront showdown. You may be shocked to learn that in 100 per cent of these situations the Advice Thruster has meekly thrown in the towel.

They are poor persuaders because they can't tell the difference between 'They agreed with me' and 'They didn't actively disagree with me'. This is at the core of most business dramas. One person spouts their one-sided viewpoint while the other patiently listens, the way one does to a racist cab driver, knowing arguing is a waste of energy. This is why those cab drivers tell you the silent majority is on their side. They don't realise why their passengers are silent.

People who are actually good at giving advice are skilled at holding up a mirror to you. They ask you lots of questions. They listen to the answers. They're sensitive to your facial expressions and vocal tone.

They ask more questions based on the signals they're noticing. They get you to voice how you feel about the situation. They essentially get you to advise yourself. It's one thing to get advice; it's another to act on it. If it's a big issue, you're unlikely to act unless you're convinced at a fundamental level, and who do you trust better than yourself?

Finding good people to give you advice is an art. If there's someone you'd love to talk to, but you feel they're too busy, famous or important to talk to you, comment on their socials first. Make a positive, thoughtful contribution and you'll get on their radar. A great tactic is to engage them on one of their non-business interests. It's more interesting to them, and makes you more memorable. After they've reacted to you a few times, message them and ask if they'd be open to answering a few questions, in person or online.

Please don't say: 'Can I pick your brain over a coffee?' I know it's just a figure of speech, but it's an ugly one and it's the universal code for 'I want high-end knowledge for $4'. Make it clear what you want to talk about. 'I would really value your advice about (a very specific topic)' will open more doors than the brain pick.

BEING DECENT
IS NOT WEAK

If you had to sort business owners and managers into categories, you could probably come up with some authoritative MBA grid. I once sat through a meeting where an eager consultant spent two hours explaining how all staff could be classified into one of four types of bird.

I think the essential split is between managers who believe people are basically decent, and those who believe people are *no damn good*. In the latter camp, all staff are lazy and stupid, and need constant direction and control. There simply aren't any good staff now, not like there used to be. Suppliers are all out to screw you, and must be screwed hard in return.

Business karma is real. If you look for the bad in every situation, bad things will come your way. People can sense you don't trust them, so you get no trust or extra effort in return. Our belief is that 99 per cent of staff are upright citizens who just want to do a good job, because doing a good job makes them proud and happy. If you treat everyone like the 1 per cent of rogue staff who falsified petty cash receipts or whatever, that's a dark place to operate from.

It's the same with suppliers. By all means, pressure them for the best deal, but it's wrong to assume that you're always the master and they the servant. Sometimes you need suppliers to help you out in a crisis, like loan a piece of vital replacement technology or send sales stock in a hurry. If you've screwed a supplier mercilessly for every penny, paid them late or returned purchases for no good reason, your favours bank is empty and those suppliers probably won't help. That can cost more than what you saved. It varies between industries, but rock-bottom purchasing shows in your product.

In our employee days, Peter and I had a business unit working inside a deluxe hotel whose general manager would, if the laws allowed, have happily made suppliers beat each other with spiked clubs in a cage until only one emerged alive. He cared only for cheap pricing. He would browbeat our staff, insult the quality of our work, and had nothing good to say about anything. When we did a particularly outstanding job, he would inspire us with a grudging, 'Well, that's what I pay you for.' We knuckled down and put up with it, because we worked for a company that could never say no. But staff turnover was horrendous and our surviving people hated their lives.

It wasn't at all like my favourite hotel in another city, a delightful, stylish place with warm, happy staff. Then came the time I stayed there and found a pall of gloom. The staff looked down and avoided eye contact, like beaten dogs. The restaurant tables had exposed cheap-ass plywood where there was once linen. There were plastic flowers. It had a grim discount funeral parlour feel. I checked in to my room, and there was the standard welcome letter from the general manager, who was . . . Mr 'That's What I Pay You For' on a new posting. I asked around industry contacts. Sure enough, occupancy in my once-favourite hotel was down and the revenue disaster of hating staff and suppliers had kicked in hard. It can take years to undo that kind of damage. Being decent to people is not weak. Sometimes you have to be tough, but don't be a total dick just because you can.

This approach applies across all your dealings, even if you're talking to strangers in a crowded room. Since our business began, we made it a rule to be nice to everyone regardless of their current commercial benefit. If you're only nice to people who are hot sales prospects, you come across as a greedy networking pimp, rolling out the smooth banter while looking over people's shoulders for someone more senior and lucrative. People can see what you're doing.

It's vital to be nice to juniors, particularly now so many clients use the Western Front Trench Warfare model of staffing: hiring battalions of keen, low-priced juniors (or worse, zero-priced interns) to charge the machine guns. When they're cut down, they replace them with fresh blood from the graduate production lines. The few survivors can get promoted quickly, and they remember who was nice to them on the way up. We have valuable clients today who remember that our people treated them with respect a few years back, when nobody else did.

It's depressing hearing business people whine about millennials. Older people seem convinced that young people have it easier than they did back in the day. Maybe it's true for some. But millennials get twice the living costs and half the job security, while being lectured on being fickle. They get more bad press for eating avocados than their parents got for eating LSD tabs. And even if millennials *were* enjoying a better life, shouldn't that be a *good thing*? If you lived in Industrial Revolution Britain, would you want your kid to become a chimney sweep because that was good enough for you?

For years, the dreaded 'How To Deal with Millennials' session was a compulsory feature at conferences. Old panellists would roll their eyes and moan about how young staff want a prize just for showing up. Changing jobs all the time! With high expectations of what they get out of a job! So high maintenance. *So* millennial. Believing that any annoying characteristic is purely down to being a millennial is delusional. Older people forget that when they were in their twenties, there was a standard bell curve of absolute stars, average workers and useless buffoons, the same as it always has been since the dawn of time. Try those 'all you people' lines but with 'Jewish people' or 'gay people' instead of 'millennials'. I'm not calling you Hitler, but you sure sound like you're in a bunker.

Nobody's asking you to employ the entire generation. The world is awash with smart, dedicated young people who just want a decent place to work. Your task is to provide that better place. That's not so hard when all you have to do is beat other places run by backwards-looking, youth-hating cranks.

SEVEN STEPS TO NO SUCCESS

I've done a lot of informal analysis over long periods on who becomes a success. You watch some get there and others battle and fail. I've listed the signs of who will make it, but you can wait until the end of the book. In the meantime, there are also some clear signs of people who won't amount to much:

1. People who don't write stuff down

I present at conferences and there are decades of ideas that I've tested with my own money, tips which can make the difference between success or failure. You see people writing them down, which is great, and you see others just staring at you, listening and letting it wash over them. They'll tell you afterwards, it's all common sense so how could they forget it? Except they do. And they take no action at all.

2. Habitual lottery ticket buyers

Everyone dreams of success. That's one of the great things that drives human progress. Lotteries allow you to outsource that dream, so 'success' comes down to a random lightning strike of luck outside your control. Why bother building your success with daily discipline and effort? The effectiveness of the lottery scam is that ticket buyers always express it as a certainty: 'When I win the lottery, I'll . . .' They won't. But should it occur, it's well documented what happens when people get a shipping container filled with dollarydoos: they spend the rest of their days dodging a family-destroying horde of scroungers. There's very little success anywhere in this system.

3. CEO of yourself

There is not much that's sadder than a business card reading 'CEO' from someone who is clearly a work-at-home solo consultant. The giveaway: the only phone number on the card is a mobile. Why not call your dog the Chief Canine Officer while you're at it? Call yourself Principal, Director or anything less grandiose than CEO.

4. People who make new year's resolutions

If you wait for a single day of the year to wake up fat, hungover and unsuccessful and then make a bunch of remedial promises you know you won't keep, that fantasy ain't happening. Successful people make plans to get stuff done on random dates like August 19th, or whatever day happens to be closest to now.

5. Mature males who have fries with their lunch

This may seem petty, but there comes a time in a man's life when he should not have fries with his lunch each day. That age is, give or take metabolic variation, twenty-five. When you see a thirty-five-year-old man in the office lunching on fried chicken and fries with a can of Coke, you know he lacks the ability to control basic, primitive urges that will turn him into a unhealthy middle-aged wreck. This ill-discipline flows into their work habits.

6. People who call their employer 'they' while talking to customers

I don't want to seem like Mister Fussy Grammar Guy but this evasive pronoun habit gives away so much. Customers want their problems sorted out. If they're talking to you, it just makes them more annoyed when you blame another part of the organisation. 'They didn't give me the information.' 'They sent me with the wrong part.' It doesn't make you look any better, it just makes the whole business look like a clown show. The worst companies on earth are the ones where nobody takes responsibility, and they just shift you from one powerless drone to another. To the earlier point about treating the business like it's your own: saying 'we', not 'they', and owning these situations is an essential sign of someone who will go places in future.

7. People who love Facebook

You're thinking: it's because it's so time-consuming and distracting, and you would be partially right. But the specific thing about Facebook is its relentless focus on the past. So much of it is 'Remember when a bag of lollies cost a penny?' and 'Who remembers playing outside in the fresh air with a ball and a stick, not with stupid phones and tablets?' and 'Remember the entertainers of our youth who had real talent, not like Kanye or that Cardi B?' That sort of backwards-looking, our-generation-is-the-best tosh. This is a really bad mindset to have in business. You should be thinking about what exciting things are next and what opportunities they will present. Nostalgia, like golf, makes you old before your time.

Not to say that any of these characteristics are evil, or mean you can't hold down a job. It just means you'll top out at middle management and all your super-success fantasies will remain just that. If you want the good stuff, it comes from years of disciplined rejection of childish distractions and weak thinking.

OBSTACLE COURSE: STOP BLOCKING YOUR OWN STAFF

Who would think so many organisations are designed to make people get less done? A quick way to lift productivity is to remove the obstacles put there by your own business.

People mostly want to do the best job they can. But many businesses are clogged by self-constructed barriers that slow them down. Rules and procedures serving no purpose, the legacy of some long-gone middle manager. Old technology that's cheap to replace. Decisions repeatedly delayed, leading to more meetings and more reports on the same issues. Salespeople spending more time filling out reports than selling.

For most businesses, staff is your single biggest expense. It's a terrifying sum every hour of every work day. Yet so many business decisions are made in an alternative universe where labour is free and the cost of the new initiative is the only variable. Someone uses $6000 in time on a plan to save $1273 a year on printer paper. Businesses make people jump through burning hoops to get a hundred dollar expense paid, but any fool manager can call pointless meetings that chew through a thousand in salaries.

It amazes me when I visit small businesses where they make their staff work on dusty beige computers with Microsoft Paperclip-era operating systems. At best, they run really slowly and at worst crash and lose an afternoon's work. The average full-time wage is about $75,000, so if they work, say, 30 per cent slower on that crappy computer, it costs you $22,000 per year in lost productivity. Plus your valuable staff spend every day physically attached to something that pisses them off. Comparatively, a new computer costs nothing: a couple of thousand, or less than 3 per cent of a salary. Why wouldn't you buy them a new one and let them work faster? You'd be the real beneficiary.

Your mission is to get all these productivity blockers out of the way. Want to know what stupid barriers your staff are facing? Commission a staff satisfaction needs analysis report and use that to develop an action plan going forward. Joking – if you think that sounds good, then *you are the problem*. Go and ask your staff yourself, now. They'll happily tell you.

Usually it's obvious, modest requests. Nobody ever asks for beer taps in the staff canteen or Swedish massages every Friday. It's always something like: 'Can I get my computer hooked up to the printer on this floor? Because otherwise I have to walk up four flights of fire-escape stairs to get each document.' There's no end to this sort of thing: stupid, time-wasting processes that exist purely due to bad software design. But the IT department is in charge, and 'That's how the system is' so staff and customers have to waste thousands of hours on workarounds, forever.

Draw up a list of everything people have asked for, then fix as many idiocies as possible immediately. Most are surprisingly affordable. The fact that you did it quickly, without more meetings, reports or capex documentation makes you look like an action hero. Your staff go: *I work in a great place*. This approach beats any pay rise or team-building activity, because after either of those two they return to the office and the daily realities grind them back down. Not saying don't give them the pay rise, but the extra-cash high wears off quickly if they still have to battle idiocies all day.

Few businesses take these simple steps, so it will make yours seem like a workers' paradise. Kick it up another notch by being prepared to say no to work. The cliché 'The customer is always right' is wrong. Most customers are wonderful and you tend to get the customers you deserve. But to believe they're always right is . . . wrong. We have had customers who have treated our valuable employees as servants, ordering them around and changing their minds with a King Louis XIV level of entitlement. This is unacceptable. Good staff are far harder to find than bad customers.

We have fired a few of these clients over the years, in a polite fashion. Not many, because, honestly, they are a tiny minority. But if you're prepared to punt a customer and their money to defend your staff it speaks volumes. It creates legends that inspire future generations of your people.

You can tell a good business by the way people *talk* to each other instead of using passive-aggressive messages. Lead by example. As soon as fights or trouble start, go to their desk or pick up the phone and sort it out. Talking it through is a remarkably quick way to get almost anything sorted out. It's not taking up space in your brain while you wait for someone to draft, redraft and send their painstaking email reply, full of assumptions and misinterpretations. Mostly, the conversation reveals that the disagreement was far smaller than you both thought and you'll part on a happy note. You'll both feel better instantly and move on to productive things for the rest of the day. Rather than stewing for hours over one badly worded line of text and thinking: 'Well, fuck you too!'

HR: A CANCER ON
YOUR BUSINESS

You've probably heard the terms 'profit centres' and 'cost centres'. Some functions in a business earn you money. Salespeople. People who make things. People who deal with customers. The more work they do, the more money the business makes. Then there are others that are Bad News Indeed for your bottom line.

Top of that list is human resources. For the small or medium business, human resources is a cancer. In that its only purpose is to multiply and metastasise at the expense of the host, your business. You hire your first human resources person and their first project is an epic slide deck on why you should hire another human resources person, due to 'increased compliance requirements'. Nobody checks if it's legit, so you end up with two of them. Then four. They stifle your whole business because they cost a lot, contribute nothing to your bottom line, and interfere with other departments' initiatives. I've seen businesses take on an HR team as a symbol of their prestigious growth. Over the first twelve months, their rates of sick leave, stress leave and everything-else leave rise to the maximum allowed.

HR brings a weird artificiality to your staff's working lives. If you don't give people immediate, direct feedback on whether they've done right or wrong, they're floating in a vacuum. People don't know if they're doing a good job or not because their sit-down appraisal isn't for months. This is madness.

At some point the HR team will ask you to rename their department 'People and Culture' or 'Optimism and Performance' or something equally deluded. If the culture of your business comes from an HR department, it's doomed to eternal mediocrity and you should resign as the leader.

A client company got a new CEO who was determined to place his stamp on the business. First on his agenda was Company Culture. So he called a meeting of key company staff. Did he address them like a leader, calling them to summon all their powers of goodness and talent to create a mighty focused force, one that will transform the industry and sweep aside all competition before it?

No, he did not.

He hired a 'Culture Consultant' to do all the talking. She set everyone up at team tables and gave them a set of items you'd use for a game at a four-year-old's birthday party. String. Pipe cleaners. Balloons. She asked everyone to work together to build something that represented 'a perfect team member'. The temptation to take the word 'member' in its Harlequin romance novel context would have been pretty strong, but career-limiting in this lunatic context.

Afterwards, a rep from each table had to stand and say what they had learnt. Because the new CEO was watching, they all had to say: 'This has been a great learning experience and I've discovered new things about myself and the company that will inspire me as I go about my daily work.'

So you get treated like a child *and* are forced to lie under oath. Good stuff, HR people.

HR likes to run constant scare campaigns about new regulatory threats to your business. Some are real, but when so many of its recommendations are based on growing their department, it's hard to judge. Part of the problem is the decline in the old-fashioned job title 'manager'. If you're a manager, you should know how the people under you are feeling, their skills, their entitlements, and how they should behave when representing your business. This is where culture comes from, not from HR people who have never done any of the actual work your business does. The worst is when a manager uses the HR department to terminate staff. If you do that, you are a contemptible, weak excuse for a leader.

We use a freelance payroll professional to make sure everyone gets paid correctly, entitlements are up to date, and all our reporting boxes are ticked. They have no direct contact with our staff at all. It works fine.

What about HR's role as someone staff can approach to discuss bullying, racism, homophobia, sexual harassment and other undesirable stuff that can go down at work? This is important. Some business owners will tell you it's political correctness gone mad, and fuck those business owners. Apart from it being basic decency, treating everyone with respect is good for your business. For the person involved, it's the single most important thing in their life at that point, so their manager has to be responsible for dealing with it, not HR. If the manager is the cause of the problem, staff have to be comfortable approaching you, the owner. If *you're* the problem, then having an HR department isn't going to help. Think of your lowest-level staff member, and ask yourself: If that person were your child, would you be happy with how their supervisor and colleagues treat them? If not, sort that shit out.

I feel a little bad writing about HR this way, thinking of dedicated HR people I know who play a legitimate role in managing their businesses, particularly ones with a large pool of casual labour. But not that bad. They would easily get jobs as managers if the whole concept of HR was put in the bin. Big businesses need HR, but SMEs should delay it for as long as you can.

The HR problem is but one symptom of Head Office Creep, a hazard for businesses that grow from small to medium. A business becomes successful, opens in multiple places, and needs some centralised functions. The theory is that instead of everyone doing their own accounts, IT, marketing, payroll and so forth, it gets centralised in one place and it costs less per office. Synergies ahoy!

Most big takeovers are justified by the idea of head office savings. Studies by people smarter and more qualified than me show this is almost never true. Once you have a head office, you end up with a CEO. I think you should have over 500 staff before you can call yourself that. CEOs like to appoint lots of departmental heads. The IT guy becomes the Chief Information Officer and so forth.

Then the empire building goes the full Donkey Kong. A task becomes a job, then that job becomes a department in no time. Other departments don't multiply to quite the same extent as HR, but managers measure their success, and future pay prospects, by the number of people under them. So they pitch for more. Then they engage consulting firms. It's purely an arse-covering exercise, because if a project goes bad, they can point to the consultant report. The IT department, fuelled by peer envy and trade show hospitality, recommends a new enterprise platform that costs as much as a fighter jet and opens the door to yet more consultants.

Your managers start calling themselves the C-Suite, a title that always makes me think of matching toilet bowl and bidet sets. I've seen head office costs go from 5 per cent to 20 per cent of revenue over a couple of years in client companies, a megalodon bite out of the margins. This doesn't escape the notice of people out there at the coalface. When one dollar in five goes to pay out-of-touch fat cats in head office, they're not going to work as hard as they once did. Now you're on the path to the trifling returns that most big companies make.

When we set up Scene Change, we deliberately didn't set up a head office. All the tasks, other than marketing and tax accounts, get handled locally. You can get casual help to do anything: bookkeepers, IT support, payroll. Local is quicker and cheaper. Of course, there are no HR people. Our people prefer direct contact with their manager, who tells it to them straight whether they're doing a good job or not, immediately. The fewer the layers of management, the better. As a result, we make margins that make us very pleased, and our people lead happier lives.

STOP SAYING
HOW BUSY YOU ARE

An anthropologist studying a herd of business people at a cocktail gathering would note they only make one sound, over and over.

'Hi, how are you? Oh, busy busy busy. So busy. Snowed under. Totally slammed. No rest for the wicked. Busy busy busy.' It's like a pond of bullfrogs, each chirping: 'Check out my cool yellow throat display.' But they all have one, so there's no competitive benefit. Only noise.

'I've been soooo busy' is as boring as saying 'It's not the heat, it's the humidity' in summer. As is asking 'How was your flight?' to anyone who's come from somewhere else. As is posting 'Today's office' if you get near a beach on a work day.

It's not an offensive thing to say. It's just what everyone else says every single time: a pure brain reflex twitch. Step one to get somewhere in the business world is distinguishing yourself from all the others identical to you. So when people say 'Hey, how's it going?' there's your golden opportunity to be interesting and charming.

Being interesting is not talking about yourself. The best way to be interesting is to *be interested*. To find out what's going on in people's lives. To learn what they're working on behind the scenes, once you dig deeper than their job title. Kicking off by saying how busy *you* are is a solid sumo wrestler blocking move that stops you learning anything about others.

172

Saying you're busy also traps the other person into having to say it too. A conversation that will never happen is:

Them: Hey, how are you?
You: Oh, *so* busy. And you?
Them: I am . . . not particularly busy.

Being face to face with an important, busy person like you, they would no sooner confess to not being busy than admit to selling Amway. So the whole busy echo chamber sustains itself. It's like that worst type of person to be around, the ones who interpret 'How are you?' as a literal invitation for the latest on their medical or personal issues. Oh God, spare us this; we do not care, we were just doing the polite verbal version of a handshake and now your colonic problems cannot be unheard.

Note that people who really *are* busy with exciting things don't say it. Because they're more in control of their own time, and being busy isn't something they regard as prestigious. Banging on about how busy you are makes you look really . . . middle management. Perhaps you have heard of the management model attributed to the 1930s German general with the outstanding name of Kurt von Hammerstein-Equord. He suggested people could be classified into a two-by-two grid with four characteristics: smart, stupid, energetic and lazy.

As a behaviour predictor, its military roots mean this model doesn't apply 100 per cent in every business, but in many workplaces it's right on the money.

According to the general, stupid and lazy people are necessary and useful. You need lots of them to get the grunt work done, and they won't cause trouble because it's too much effort.

Smart and energetic people are very useful most of the way up the career ladder, for implementing plans and ensuring that every detail gets properly considered. But they won't get to the top because they get too involved.

Smart and lazy people are incredibly valuable. They'll sit back and work out the best ways to get the other three quadrants working. They have 'the requisite nerves and mental clarity for difficult decisions' and enough spare time to think things through. He advised they should be promoted to the highest level.[6]

Energetic and stupid people are the absolute worst. They come up with stupid plans, then waste everyone's time trying to make them a reality. *These* are the people who tell you they're busy all the time. This is the Dunning–Kruger heartland: the classic psychological syndrome of thick people being more confident, because they're not bright enough to recognise their own limitations.

What should you say instead? You don't need a *line*. LinkedIn success grifters think you need some elevator pitch line that you've practised alone in the bathroom mirror for hours like some friendless psychopath. It's the approach of deluded guys in nightclubs, with memorised lines they read in pick-up books. They have lots of short, unsuccessful conversations. If 'conversation' is the right word when one of the people involved only says one word, and that word is 'No'.

Sure, you need a clear, interesting answer when someone says 'Tell me about your business', but that's not how you open a conversation. I get people introducing themselves with: 'Hi I'm James from Evently we're the one-click solution for digital event planning.' And I'm thinking: Calm down, James, this feels like when you visit someone's house and their dog starts jumping all over you as you step through the door.

Just say: 'I'm great, thanks. What have you been up to?' Listen. And take it from there. Say things like 'That sounds cool, tell me more.' And 'Where do you think it's going?' Practise open questioning technique, not elevator pitches, until it becomes part of your personality. They will remember you. In a good way. You'll never need to use the b-word again.

7.

FINANCE

I'M RICH:
DEAL WITH IT

Sorry for the boast, but I've been rolling in it for quite a while. It's awesome fun – you should definitely try it. Right now you're thinking: this is a dummy opener, he's about to say he's rich in the love of his family and friends, the greatest wealth of all. No, I am not about to say that; this is not the book for sappy fridge-magnet wisdom. I'm talking about sweet cash. And material possessions. Damn, it makes me happy, and I don't care if you think I'm birdbath-shallow.

Want to know how to get rich like me? And are you sure you want to keep reading after that sleazy pitch line? Okay, I'll let you in on the secret. It all comes down to your definition of being rich. Here's mine:

It's when you reach that point when you don't have to worry about money all the time.

You can do that with heaps less money than you imagine. Where I am is a massive leap from when I *was* worried about money all the time, and I'm really grateful for that. Worrying about money takes up entire lobes of your brain all day. Once you get to that no-worries point, it's up to you whether you behave like an adult. The easiest way to make a dollar is to *not* spend it on escalating lifestyle and stupid success props.

The popular image of business success is all Lamborghinis and Hermès handbags. These are the aspirations of *Love Island* contestants, not well-balanced business people. You don't need a gold helicopter and a valet to launder your mink underpants. Prestige products are designed to suit people much better-looking than you or me. You might think you look like Daniel Craig vaulting into the Aston Martin, but in reality you look like Clive Palmer outside court, battling to squeeze under the gullwing doors on his Benz.

Also, Ferraris and Lamborghinis are slow cars. Yes, they're quick on an open road. But that advantage is more than offset by other drivers not letting sportscar dickhead merge into traffic, so you arrive later. Want everyone to let you ahead with a wave and a smile every time? Drive my business partner's old red VW dune buggy. They're reasonably priced, and you'll be like the happiest character in *Mario Kart*.

I put a new battery in my three-year-old iPhone because it's fine and phones are all the same now. If we took our business to IPO I would still send the kids into the supermarket to buy snacks for the movies, because those $12 boxes of popcorn and $7 waters can fuck right off. I assume you have to inherit your money to get that sort of entitled, DGAF approach to business and life expenses. But it is very pleasant to not have to worry what your restaurant bill is going to be. And to be able to splash out on the occasional treat when you have totally earned it: specifically, Pol Roger Cuvée Sir Winston Churchill champagne, humanity's peak alcohol achievement.

I once spent an apartment-deposit amount of money on chemo-therapy for my daughter's beloved Burmese cat, Max. I know everyone thinks their pet is pretty good, but this one was the real deal. All the staff at the vet hospital, from the assistants to the cat professors, would say: 'Damn, that is one charismatic cat.'

If the businesses weren't working, or if I had a job with a modest salary, he'd have been put down well before his time. When you have money, you can choose to escalate your cat's treatment to epic levels. If I had to choose between sinking a pile of money into keeping Max above ground or a new car, it's the cat in a heartbeat. The standard response is: 'Are you out of your goddamn mind? That much? On a *cat*?'

I don't have to care what you think. It may not be your choice. But to *have* the choice is better than waving an early goodbye to a trusty beast you love. These are the things that will make you tingle at a far deeper level than a Rolex or another pair of Louboutins.

I'm not saying my way is the only way. A friend just bought a mad US muscle car as a reward for turning his business around from tax-debt basket case to profitable growth story. The prospect of that car inspired him through some dark times. Now ten people have good jobs with him and that is brilliant. Whatever gets you there. I'm delighted if you can buy a giant harbourfront home, because if you've earned that money then you can spend it however the hell you want. Though just the thought of having to manage all those gardeners gives me a headache.

Beyond not spending the money, starting your own business really helps. It removes the hourly rate cap on how much money you can make. It also clarifies the way you look at finances. Because by the time you get there, you'll know how hard it is to actually get and keep money. So you can't snap out of cost-control mode after years of it being second nature. My business partners will go into battle over some $17 overcharge, not because we need $17, but because screw you for trying to overcharge us.

When you're on a salary, the cash flow is much more dependable. You work hard so you can get a raise, then when you get it, you celebrate by ratcheting your spending habits up so you're no better off. You just have more rooms in your success house that need to be furnished and cleaned.

If you keep your living costs low, you can make decisions without fear because your prestige car repayments or school fees aren't threatened. Paradoxically, you make a lot more money if you're not scared about losing it. That's because business success is largely about your ability to make a quick decision and move on. Modest living costs are an amazing force field as you head out onto the business battlefield. The bullets and explosions bounce off while you wander around in a relaxed state of mind.

While being rich is cool, it's easy to forget what it was like before. Rich people start thinking everyone feels like them. You see it when they talk about motivation at work.

'The money isn't important. There are so many other levels of experience, peer recognition and self-actualisation that outweigh remuneration.'

Anyone who says this is absolutely loaded and has completely forgotten what it was like when the money was *really fucking important*. Try that cosmic chat with a single parent raising kids on a casual wage, living in fear of opening her credit card statement and discovering the five-year-old clocked up $3000 of in-app purchases when she gave him the phone to stop the screaming from the back seat. Try telling the young casual teacher who has no choice but to drive to work and the tollways take the first two hours of their wage each day.

Money is life-or-death important for them. If they're your staff or customers, don't be patronising them with your rich-person Dalai Lama routine.

Visualising successful Future You is an essential technique. But by definition, it's much easier to picture visual things. So you see yourself at the Mercedes dealership picking up the keys from a fawning sales manager. Or checking into the El Presidente Grande Suite with your matching Vuitton luggage. Those are vivid, sexy-ass images.

The real pleasures of getting there are much harder to picture. How do you visualise *not* having to run expensive new projects past a tight-arsed CFO? Instead, it's a quick phone hookup with your business partners who say: 'Yeah, let's do it right now.' How do you picture finding someone young and promising, recognising their potential where others didn't, giving them the freedom to try and fail, and five years on they're running part of your business better than you could?

Or indeed, the pleasure of having time to write a book, rather than having meetings all day. I'm not rich like people on rich lists, but what I do have is control over my own time and zero outside interference. I'm a freakin' mogul in terms of freedom to do what the hell I like. Often that's something to do with the businesses, but that's my choice and I love it.

These are abstract pleasures, hard to visualise. ('Close your eyes. Breathe deeply. I want you to see yourself sitting on a couch with a laptop for six hours writing lines that suck, then deleting them. WOOOO YEAHHH SUCCESS!') Yet for most of us, these are the things that make business life a deeply rewarding experience.

TOP FIVE SAYINGS OF THE FINANCIALLY ILLITERATE

Wondering how to tell if someone you're hiring or doing business with has any understanding of finance? It's amazing how many people rise high without much awareness of how all them fancy numbers work. Sometimes it isn't practical to make them sit a financial literacy test.

I've done a lot of chin-scratching with managers who are loss-making machines, taking a business model that's profitable elsewhere and using it to burn bales of cash. As a writer I'm sensitive to words and as a business owner I'm sensitive to people losing our money. Reconcile the two and you notice phrases those managers use again and again. They're a Code Red warning you're better off putting your precious capital coin by coin into an amusement arcade claw machine and hoping to pick up a profitable quantity of fluffy toys. Learn from my pain.

1. 'You have to spend money to make money'

This is true. Many businesses fail to make money because they're run by Scrooges who starve their staff of the tools to do their job. You need to spend money, on capex, marketing and the best staff you can get.

But the people who do these things successfully *never* say: 'You have to spend money to make money.'

The people who *do* say it . . . just like to spend money. They get a near-sexual buzz from buying things: designer office furniture, domestic business-class air travel, prestige cars on novated leases ('It would actually have been more expensive to keep my old car') and stupid status credit cards with a four-figure annual fee. They have drug-lord expense habits, and when you query them, they trot out the old faithful phrase.

Nothing they like to spend money on will actually make your business any money.

2. 'Tax-deductible'

There are many bogus parallels drawn between personal finance and business finance. Plank-thick politicians speak of debt as 'putting it on the national credit card', as if worthy nation-building investments using record-low interest rates are the same as drunk-buying a second Nutribullet on your Visa at 23 per cent.

Someone will pitch you an idea that needs money – often it's sponsorship of their brother's speedway car – and they finish with the clincher: '. . . and it's fully tax-deductible!' They are convinced that tax-deductibility has some kind of triple-bonus multiplier effect that will make everyone wads of cash.

'You mean it's an expense?' you say.

'Not only that, it's tax-deductible.'

If you can't understand that the more 'tax-deductible' things you buy, the lower your profit, you are 100 per cent employment-deductible.

3. 'Good for tax losses'

This is a longer-term gambit from the same people who say 'tax-deductible', as if tax losses are some kind of awesome ongoing business model. It carries the same secretive multimillionaire imagery as the words 'Caymans' and 'blind trusts'. Sure, you can use tax losses as a consolation for the worst of your screw-ups and failed experiments, but at some point you need profit to offset them against. Many people believe the losses are the main game.

4. 'I'm doing a bit of day trading'

Not much says 'unemployable' like telling people you're doing some day trading. Pro traders working for global firms with huge research resources still find it hard to beat the index. People sitting around at home in their underpants clutching a book'n'DVD kit called *Make Million$ Day Trading* are no different to chronic racetrack gamblers. I've never seen anyone who admits to dabbling in day trading turn out to be anything but an eternal career drifter, moving from one disappointing scheme to another. It's a clear sign they cannot be trusted to do anything with your money other than lose the lot.

5. 'A million dollars' worth'

From time to time we run the tape measure over an acquisition. You check out a business someone has built up through decades of back-breaking effort. Usually, it provides enough cash to keep the owner and their family in a job. Profit left after they're paid: zero.

So you ask them how much they want and they say they'd like One Million Dollars or whatever they need to sit on a banana lounge drinking sav blanc for the rest of their life. There are only two basic ways to value a business: as a multiple of its profit, or the value of its assets. So, you ask them, given that the multiple of zero profit is, ah, zero, what do you think that warehouse full of assets is worth?

'There's a million dollars' worth.'

Oh no there isn't. Much of it is old, weathered and out of date. Some of it has resident possums.

'Do you mean that over the last ten years, you've paid a total of a million dollars for that stuff? Mostly over five years ago?' you ask.

'That's right. A million dollars' worth.'

It's amazing how many people are so in love with every object they buy that they can't imagine it ever being worth a penny less than the day their trembling hands first unpacked it. So to offer them under One Million Dollars for their business is a slap in the face to them and the assets they hold dear. Obviously, they will never sell their business. There's a strong chance they'll be entombed in it like a pharaoh, surrounded by their precious things: Compaq laptops, fax machines and Palm Pilot digital assistants.

TRUST OTHER PEOPLE TO USE YOUR MONEY

It's a major leap of faith to give a manager in a different city a fat pile of your cash and hope they won't spend it on personal travel, three-hat restaurant meals or gambling chips. Yet you must if you're to experience the buzz of earning money from a business you don't work in.

Yes, you can do audits. You can check the figures all you like. But if your business partners are really keen to stick their paws in the cookie jar, there are ways they can do it on a minor scale and you'll never know. You have to find people who are honest, and trust them. Some business owners in our field are bewildered by how we can place that faith in people and still sleep at night. But dishonest people, like random paedophiles in vans, are nowhere near as common as mythology suggests.

Plus the sort of people who put their personal habits on the company tab are also disorganised, so they eventually leave a trail. This is another reason to start a business a bit later in life. You've worked with more grifters and scoundrels, so your detective instincts are better tuned.

Are our partners getting the best possible returns with our money? In our case, it helps that as shareholders it's their money at risk too. Sometimes they'll do worse with the business than we would have. Mostly they'll do better. But if you're going to breathe down their necks and tell them what to do, you may as well be managing the business yourself. That caps both your potential growth and your enjoyment on the whole journey.

In the first few years, when everyone's learning and mistakes are more likely, you have to let them take a long run on the line. It'll test your faith. Your instincts will say: pull them up before they fail. But you have to let them do it. Our business partners call us up and describe some difficult issue, and the correct response is the most essential management line there is: 'What do *you* think you should do?' They're usually right, but the act of saying their plan out loud helps them clarify it.

Don't jump in with your own ideas. You might steer them a bit. But don't tell them *exactly* what to do. We have deliberately let people make expensive mistakes with our money purely for the long-term educational value. They have to earn their degree at the University of Pain.

People don't really learn when you tell them precedents, lists or what *you* would have done. Those things aren't memorable enough. A good story helps, if it's relevant and well told. But nothing beats them sticking their hand on the hot frying pan and learning how that feels. Once is enough for most people. You can tell good people by how quickly they learn from pain.

I've worked with people who have taken horrific metaphorical burns, checked out of casualty with bandaged hands, gone straight into the kitchen to see a smoking pan on the stove and thought: I wonder what that feels like? Over and over. Some people are on a six-monthly or annual cycle of pain, learning, achievement, then . . . forgetfulness and more pain.

If you take the 'I'm always right' approach, you'll attract the sort of manager better suited to running a mall doughnut franchise. There are few surprises to deal with in that context. But if you want innovation and cunning at a local level, you need entrepreneurial hustlers. They don't want you to be standing over them with a franchise rule book going, 'Refer to page 125, paragraph 9.'

An interesting financial secret: we have achieved continuous growth and profitability without once setting a budget. Not one. We have never asked a manager to set a revenue target, or given them one. This approach makes MBAs and most managerial types squirm. How on earth can you run a business without the most basic, essential management tool of all? Surely that sort of free-form anarchy must destroy shareholder value and leave everyone adrift without a map. Calm down, white-shirt people.

Budget-worship comes from the big-corporate mentality that predictability is more important than actual results. They would rather make a steady 5 per cent profit every year than make 25 per cent one year, 2 per cent the next, and 16 per cent the year after. It keeps the analysts calm, but spreads a sandbagging mentality throughout the business. Middle managers manipulate their targets down to avoid blame. Upper management hands down unachievable growth targets that make staff do stupid, unsustainable deals. Capex money gets spent on follies because there was budget left. None of this is good for your business.

Imagine we set a budget for our partners and they failed to reach it. What exactly are we going to do? Send them to their rooms? We put a lot of time into gathering a team we trust to chase every bit of revenue and minimise every cost they can. We know they're always doing their best.

You don't have to use every method from business school just because they worked for General Electric. If budgets make you feel comfortable, go for it, but with the right sort of manager, internal drive will always beat external commands. So you'll need people with at least a decade of solid industry experience with contacts, deal-pursuit skills and the ability to think for themselves. Better they go a bit outside the guidelines in a quest for innovation than wait for orders. It's interesting to see the long-term effects of head office constraint on good people.

We've seen it in a few business partners we've liberated from other companies, where employers or partners kept them in total information darkness. One was a minority equity partner in a similar business. The other partner never showed him any of the figures. Not a single P&L, balance sheet or bank statement. It was like a blindfold party game. The guy was managing the business but was only given ratios to work with, once a quarter. He knew the revenue but he had no idea how his day-to-day actions affected profit.

Occasionally, extra money would land in his personal bank account, which could have been a bonus, a dividend or maybe a laundered inheritance from an exiled Nigerian prince. He never knew. If you're in that sort of situation, you're in real danger of waking up one day and finding your partner has moved to the Canary Islands, leaving you with all the debt in the world. You sign a lot of documents when you own a business, many of them as you're running out the door late for a meeting. Without partners you trust like family, there is no telling what you could be liable for.

I mentored a friend who had equity in a business. I asked her if there was a shareholder contract. She couldn't remember signing one. Share certificates? She didn't think so. She hunted through her laptop. Turns out what she had was an email from the boss saying 'You have 20 per cent equity in the business'. That is . . . not a shareholding. There was no malice or evil intended; they were just super-busy people who hadn't got to the paperwork in two years. If your company takes off unexpectedly and sells for a fortune, your 'IOU Shares' email isn't worth the paper it's not even written on.

Cost-control skills are right up there on the essential skills list. You want people who feel the pain of expenses. You see them look at the price of something and there's a slight biting of the lower lip, a furrowing of the brow, because it gives them physical discomfort. You need that. Others simply go through the purchasing process with a wide-eyed happy panda expression, spinning your cash out the door with gusto. And before long, you too will have to subsist on a diet of bamboo leaves.

SWEET CASH: GET IT, KEEP IT

Apologies in advance: this chapter is a bit accounts-y. But it's about cash, which you want, so stick with it. Here's how it works. Healthy businesses have cash. Unhealthy ones are always behind. Unless you're a VC-funded tech startup, which is the cash version of getting into your parents' liquor cabinet at age seventeen. Cash is the only true KPI, and until it's in your bank account, you have more work to do.

If you run out of cash, you have to shut the doors, and you might get disqualified as a company director. A question you should be able to answer roughly off the top of your head at all times is: what's your bank balance plus Accounts Receivable (what you're owed) less Accounts Payable (what you owe right now)? If you can't answer it, you probably shouldn't own a business.

Those numbers, along with your sales numbers for the next few months, should influence your behaviour all day. Should you allow that new customer credit or ask for cash up front? Should you buy that new laptop? If you're not across those four numbers, you're driving without headlights. Plenty of business owners don't know these basics, and say, 'My accountant handles all of that for me,' like they're too important to know. Dead business walking.

Aside from pricing too low and loose credit terms, a major source of cash trouble is treating the business like your own ATM. Your rookie thinks 'net profit' equals the amount of money they can take out of the business now. No, paws off. As a general law principle, you can't pull dividends out until you declare a profit in your end-of-year figures. Laws aside, it's also a good idea to keep your outfit healthy.

Experienced operators will tell you to roughly divide your profit by three. A third will go in company tax. A third should be reinvested in the business. And the other third you should usually take out for yourself. See how most useful business rules are chimp-simple?

If you ignore putting money aside for tax, it's a swift death spiral. Once it gets away from you it's incredibly hard to catch up through regular trading, because more trading means owing even more tax. We got into this exciting position in our early, heavy-capex years, where every cent of income went to fuel growth.

If you fall behind on tax, here's what you do: call the Tax Office as soon as possible and tell them your problems. They are generally pretty reasonable. They are so used to scams and denials that if you tell them straight what's going on, they will usually strike a deal. So you can pay off your larger tax debt in smaller instalments over time, while staying on top of new tax debts. Be grateful for the let-off and take this obligation very seriously. If you don't 'fess up and they find out – and they will – you'll get fines to add to your crushing burden. Then you have one nostril above the alligator-infested swamp, on a rising tide.

If you don't reinvest the third back into the business, you're running it down to a hollow shell. That's okay if it suits your personal circumstances to suck all the cash out now, like if you're about to retire. If you're buying a business, look carefully to see if that's what the seller is up to. You buy what you believe to be a working business and then discover it's a worn-out relic, and now you must pay for expensive renovations.

Finally the exciting third, the part you get to pull out and spend on well-earned goodies for yourself. This is hard in the early growth years, but once your business is past the five-year mark, don't make it optional. Pull money out. Otherwise, what is the point of having a business? The alternative is hoarding it all for long-term growth, but it means all your wealth is tied up in the business. That's risky. Maybe you can sell it later, but it's not guaranteed.

The ability to sell your business moves in a slow cycle in any given sector. About once a decade, big companies go on a wild debt-fuelled spree and they'll buy *anything* in your category. There's a lot of pig lipstick applied at these times. Keep saying things like 'globally scalable business model' and you might get lucky. Then the purchase pyramid collapses and it goes quiet for another ten years.

If you want to sleep at night, the best way to manage cash is to set up multiple accounts. A daily cash account and a tax savings account. You split off the tax money as client payments come in. Feel free to have more accounts, depending on what uses you have for cash. You'll have a much clearer idea of where you sit. You don't get that morale-killing feeling when money you thought was yours actually belongs to the government.

If you're thinking of buying into an existing business, here's what matters: net profit and cash flow. The further from these excellent basic measurements you go, the more it says: Something To Hide. Like when the seller speaks mainly of EBITDA, which measures earnings without considering a bunch of real costs. EBITDA is largely a measure of how the company would be performing if it were a different company in a parallel universe where cash flow wasn't important. As an exciting experiment, try asking a restaurateur if they'll take EBITDA to settle up your meal. Stay out of knife range.

Cash aside, how do you know what shape your business is in? We spoke of sticking to a few essential ratios before. If you try to make everything important, nothing's important.

If you're new at this, you might wonder, what are the right percentages for your industry? Local competitors won't tell you. This is where the International Secret League of Business Owners comes into it. Travel to other countries (when you're allowed) and have dinner with successful owners in the same game. If you have a salaried job, you'll never know of this camaraderie between business owners. We're pretty open with each other about figures, not because we want to boast, but because that's what we're interested in. And we respect others who have taken risks. Being Australian just makes it easier: people seem to pre-like us before they've had a chance to judge our actual character, and they tell you everything. It's enormous fun and you'll make some lifelong friends.

Another option is to find advisers. I do it for a few businesses. It's helpful for solo business owners, because it's good to have someone marking your homework. To make it work, you need to be producing hard numbers, like you're reporting to a board.

If you actually *are* reporting to a board, keep it short and to the point. I'm a words guy. That's how you create the vision for your staff and customers. But for board reporting, I want as few words as possible. I'd like specific, unarguable numbers. Too many words are a warning that there's something to hide.

Don't say *strong growth*, give us a number. Don't say *premium pricing strategy*, tell us what extra percentage you're charging over competitors. Don't say *committed staff*, give us staff turnover numbers. *Well-positioned for market turnaround* says your fixed costs are too high. Your LinkedIn bio might be 'Storyteller-In-Chief' but please spare us your J. K. Rowling work in reports. Each adjective makes your report weaker and more suspicious.

Committing to putting those numbers together at least every two months is a vital discipline. So is explaining them to other people. You don't actually understand something until you can explain it clearly to others. If your numbers are bad you'd better have a decent explanation of how you're going to fix it.

I like to see the bad news. Good news is good, but it kinda looks after itself. Good managers can see bad things coming and work on a plan. Some managers think presenting a sanitised package of good news makes them look professional. 'It's all good,' they chirrup, until the figures show the Apocalypse is at hand. You should have been acting on the causes six months ago and now everything's on fire.

I'm not sure which are worse, the managers who hide bad news or the ones who don't even know it's there. Either option makes me want to clap their head between two saucepan lids.

YOU DON'T NEED
LAWYERS UNTIL YOU DO

Lawyers will tell you most people's idea of how law works is formed by watching *Suits*.

There's conflict. Then a tense boardroom stand-off between opposing parties. All the female lawyers have long, glossy hair, tossed around to underline the tension. Voices are raised, leather compendia slammed shut, someone storms out. Then many dead ends until a solitary lawyer, working late in a canyon of files, finds a document that proves the case Beyond Reasonable Doubt. They stroke their chin. The music sting plays as we cut to their court arrival the next morning, in a fresh suit with a knowing look on their face.

The whole case is wrapped up in satisfying style within the allocated hour. Every week. Guess what: it's not like that. Particularly with business matters. It's slow, there's no shouting, and it doesn't usually end with the clear-cut high-five win. It's more of a compromised, thank-God-that's-over sort of finale. Plus now your lawyer dresses the same as you, in grocery-shop casual.

If you bring a TV-conflict mentality to your commercial affairs, you'll have no business in quick time. Here's the deal with lawyers when you're starting out. You can't afford them. You can't afford anything. But you need some basic lawyering. Golden Law Rule: immunisation is better than cure.

193

Getting stuff properly documented is a vital investment against future evil. It's not so much the document details, it's the fact that you have them documented in the first place. Having someone sign a legal document is like an electric fence for farm animals. Once activated, it doesn't always have to be switched on to keep their behaviour in line.

To keep trouble at bay, you will need customer terms and conditions. Start by looking at someone else's terms and conditions in your field. Run a lawyer through the parts that suit you and have them plug the gaps you didn't know existed. You can't just do a Find/Replace Name edit on your competitor's terms and conditions. Apart from the risk of leaving legal holes, it's a copyright infringement. (You thought copyright only applied to things that are nice to read, didn't you? 'Original work' sounds like art. Sorry, the dullest list of dot points about rental-car return penalties can still be an original work by some poor bastard, protected under the law.)

You'll need staff contracts. They cost a bit up-front, and you wonder how important they are, given all your staff are awesome and love working for you. Surely none of them will rat you out for some accidental error. Sooner or later, one of them will. You hire a lawyer who breaks the news that you misread an award detail five years ago. You've been short-paying everyone the whole time, and now you owe half a million dollars back pay. Pay issues have the largest potential to come back and bite you on the bum. I've seen it happen and it can be terminal.

If you have partners, you'll need a shareholder contract. There's a popular idea that you use lawyers to create a giant, murky contract with clauses hidden on page 73 designed to screw one party. Three years on: 'Ha! Under clause 97.3.b you forfeit your firstborn child for your failure to deliver on said deliverables.'

This is absolutely the case if your situation involves Queensland real estate. Or if you're a small supplier dealing with a giant customer. Their contract will not be to your advantage. Your lawyer's job is to explain in simple terms that your big new customer would like to keep you down a black, greasy pit, lowering just enough food and water once a day to keep you alive, so you can attend to their dark needs for the contracted period. You can send that customer suggested amendments, and their answer will be 'Lol'.

Then it's your call whether it's worth the risk. Basically all of business is making calls about whether things are worth the risk. I know people down that huge-customer pit. They really have no choice but to bite down on the squash ball for years on end.

In regular business, most contracts aren't things you win or lose, they're just the needs of both parties written down so you're covered for future situations. So everyone can chill out and get on with their lives. I wrote our original shareholder contracts, editing templates I found online. They were six pages long and clocked in at Year 8 on the readability index. They included points like:

> The shareholders acknowledge that the primary purpose of the business is creating a long-term (at least ten years) privately-held source of income with a minimum of corporate posturing. It is not being set up for a quick sale or IPO, as none of the shareholders wish to serve another three-year term of employee servitude under evil external owners who don't understand this industry. Shareholders should arrange their affairs accordingly.

You can tell we were all a bit gun-shy after a close brush with private equity. My DIY work was adequate at the time, but you should not do it. It was based on our view that the spirit of the document is important. This was a statement of intent between people who like and respect each other. Our mission was to avoid the crushing bureaucracy we'd experienced elsewhere. That contract was a reflection of that nimble goal, and that's what our business became. But I've also seen close friendships in other businesses torn apart. Get a lawyer to write you a basic contract. It brings the extra value of being covered by their professional indemnity insurance should things turn ugly.

In our first decade, we took pride in not using lawyers for anything other than checking contracts. We handled all the adversarial work ourselves. If you have to pay lawyers to do your fighting, you need better negotiation skills.

Also, all the lawyers I'd ever dealt with were complete roadblocks to progress. You propose a deal or strategy. They present a long list of reasons why you should not act. Every goddamn time. Because of some obscure 'what if' possibility that *might* cost something further down the track.

They were unconcerned about money *not* made because you followed their advice to do nothing. If those lawyers had their way, there would be no workplace accidents or road toll, because everyone would sit indoors wearing padded sumo suits, never venturing out into the world of potential risks. I always wondered where they thought the money that pays their bills comes from, given their eternal preference for blocking deals.

Then I was asked to sit on the advisory board of a law firm just as COVID-19 was gathering momentum. I'd hoped it was in recognition of my legal academic work, the sum total of which is my Theory of Eyewear Phrenology. I believe you can determine the guilt of the accused purely by the sunglasses they wear for the media walk outside court. Under my system, the judge reviews media footage, notes the defendant's servo-rack Oakley knock-offs, and simply says: 'I find you Guilty As Fuck.' You know it's true and it would unclog the courts.

Turns out the firm only does big business law so my theory must wait. On the upside, law is really interesting. Turns out there are lawyers with strong commercial instincts; I just hadn't met them until now. Their approach is to sort out the situation using all the tools available, and law might be one of those.

That was handy, because out of nowhere came our Year Of The Lawpocalypse. You don't need lawyers until you do. A government department declared random war on one of our businesses, trying to shut it down for doing something that thousands of similar businesses do. A client screwed us to the tune of over $10 million. There's more I can't talk about because it's still going. All on top of having most of our businesses shut by the pandemic. Suddenly, our world was awash with lawyers. Despite the stress of wondering if all your businesses will die, it's an exhilarating feeling having people with really powerful brains in your corner, who know law but are also smart business people. You, the client, have instincts, but there are times when you should shut up and let the experts take the wheel.

At least one of our businesses would be in the morgue if not for our lawyer's calm tactical guidance through a saga of exasperating bullshit. How do you find a good one? The usual: ask others if they know a non-roadblock lawyer who understands business. People make all the jokes about lawyers wanting to smash you with as many billable hours as possible. The sort of lawyer you want is not amped to take on work that stems from your own stupidity and disorganisation, no matter how lucrative. They have better things to do. They would rather work for less time to get you organised than save your chaotic arse from preventable trouble later.

Suggestion: talk to your lawyer and ask them what causes the most problems and preventable legal actions in your field. I'll take a stab in the dark and suggest a Top 3. It'll be your sales staff not making it clear what customers can expect for their money. Haphazard credit granted to customers who should pay up front. And one business partner going rogue on the solitary decisions without the others knowing. If you know the warning signs, you can act on the causes before things get legal.

It helps to know some law yourself. Not to a lawyer level, but general knowledge will make you better at business. Start with the Competition and Consumer Act. Being in business without knowing what's in there is like driving a truck without a licence or having read the road rules. You can harm yourself and others. I know plenty of business people blissfully unaware they're breaking laws all over the place, some from other bits of legislation. Things like running contests that may need a permit. Taking undisclosed commissions. Making customers sign waivers, thinking it voids their legal obligations. Naughty, expensive when you get caught, and ignorance is no defence.

Fringe benefit: it helps in your own consumer situations, where you're trying to return a dodgy product and the store is refusing to take responsibility. You go: 'Look, I get that your "policy" is no returns, but your laminated sign there doesn't override your legal responsibilities, mate. Section 54 of the Australian Consumer Law says: goods have to be fit for all the purposes for which goods of that kind are commonly supplied. And this kettle is *very* far from that.'

They infer from this knowledge that you are a lawyer. They have seen lawyers on TV, so they're not going to be able to bluff their way through this one.

Sure, it's a next-level Karen move, but also, screw those people. They must not win.

PAY YOUR TAX

So many business people are obsessed with tax, as if tax is the sole input and output of their business, and their entire success depends on how many shonky tax credits they can claim.

That's all they talk about with other business people. They whine about how they're single-handedly saving the country with their crippling tax contributions, yet they have no say in how it's spent. The money goes to things they specifically dislike: gruel subsidies for orphans, grants to artists whose work isn't even a recognisable picture of anything, and the biased uncommercial thinking of scientists.

But obsessing about tax distracts you from your business when it should be a fringe issue. Your tax hater says: 'I'm paying a heap of tax! It's a disaster and I'm so unhappy.' But wouldn't a better state of mind be: 'I'm paying heaps of tax and that's great because that means my business is making epic profits and I get to keep most of it. Life is good!'

Most of the cunning tax schemes are gone now, unless you're a multinational, in which case you just tick the 'Opt Out of Tax' box on your return. As a regular one-country business there's not much you can do. All your worrying, complaining and tax scheming might lower your tax bill a bit. But if you put that energy into your clients and building your business, you'll get a better return.

199

I'm not saying pay more tax than you have to. We ask our accountants to minimise our tax within the conventional rules like family trusts. But we pay a stack of tax every month and we're okay with that. We like the handy roads that our trucks drive on and the reliable water and power supplies that our tax helps provide.

Tax is not something we can change. Tax haters become so obsessed that they start believing the government is the source of all their problems. The government should do this and that. It doesn't support business the way Gold Coast wine guy demands. It's a dangerous mentality. You start thinking there's nothing you can do until the government gives you favours. When you believe someone else controls your success or failure, you lose the glorious entrepreneur ability to feel in total control of your own destiny. Even though it's only in their minds, these people are as much controlled by government as any subsidised French micro-farmer.

Taken to the ultimate extent, your tax hater will move to Bermuda or some other shonky bolthole, which becomes its own punishment. A life spent in yacht clubs surrounded by other greedy evasive tossers like yourself, far from family, friends, culture and any sense of home, talking about how much tax you've saved and complaining about boat maintenance costs. If you think that will make you happy, go straight to a psychologist and sort your priorities out.

A decision based purely on tax is a bad decision, morally *and* commercially. My first business kicked off quickly, due to charging my normal rates, but in US dollars at a 47.5 cent exchange rate. Each client payment filled my bank account like the Hoover Dam. I'd never seen anything like it in my employee days. I was at a crossroads. Tradition dictated that as a creative director suddenly flush with funds, I should buy a Porsche and hit the nose beers. My inner actuary said: No, get a financial planner and invest for the future. So I asked conservative finance industry friends for recommendations. From that list I picked the most sensible, bespectacled, city-officed financial planner I could find.

He said that for tax reasons, I should invest in the same things he had invested in personally. So I put the bulk of my money into a managed citrus plantation with elite tax benefits and a geared share portfolio to turbocharge my stock market returns. I put that in the mental box marked 'sorted' and went back to decisions I was interested in. After a few years, the spider senses started tingling as I sent yet another six-figure payment to the still-unproductive citrus badlands. The numbers were poor. The reports used the same sayings as every dud company annual report: 'Tougher than expected conditions'; 'Unexpected head-winds'; 'Poised for growth when world prices recover'. Turns out 'I've invested in this personally' is another Code Red financial alert.

Finally realising it was an irredeemable dog, I tried to get out. Of course, there were no buyers. I rode it to the end, still obliged to cough up huge chunks of 'tax-effective' money as the scheme appeared more frequently in business media, then the general news. When that happens, you know you're screwed. At least I hadn't borrowed money to feed that beast. I went to investor meetings full of tearful old couples with massive debts for an investment worth zero.

The geared share portfolio was heavy on finance wizard compa-nies like Babcock & Brown that all died in the GFC. I dumped what wreckage was left, along with the financial planner. I burnt a house-sized amount of money in that caper.

Bad luck. Don't invest money unless you're prepared to lose it all. Since then I've spent a lot of time weeding out financial planner commissions in all sorts of secret corners of my affairs. Super funds, insurance policies, all wired up with trailing commission codes sending cash back to that guy forever in exchange for no work. The level of the scam is breathtaking. Surprises are still popping up like unexploded mines, a decade on.

You learn that any scheme designed for tax minimisation attracts weasels. Turns out financial planners got large chunks of those invest-ments as up-front kickbacks. Rivers of easy money for weasels means they go out and plant more trees. Not the number of trees that suits the amount of oranges and lemons people want to buy, but the number of trees that thousands of dentists want tax-deducted. The scheme opera-tors get less picky about the land they use, and they don't need to worry themselves sick about operating costs like regular farmers. They have all sorts of non-farmer management who would be hard pressed to pick out oranges from lemons in an identity line-up.

So a massive fruit oversupply grown with a fat cost structure hits the market, prices plunge and hey, who could have seen that coming? The only winners are the Lords of the Weasel Kingdom, the liquidators who sit astride the carcass for years, customising their fee strategy to ensure every remaining cent goes to them.

Invest in real businesses, pay your tax, take pride in being a useful member of society and you will be a happier, better person.

NO CREDIT FOR YOU, SCUMBAG

Giving customers credit is like habitually using a hair dryer in the bath. You know how to hold a hair dryer. You've done it a thousand times. But you only have to drop it in the bath once. There is no business topic with such a galactic gap between what people know they should do versus their actual behaviour.

You can create a winning business over years of dedicated work and the whole lot can be brought down by one bad debt, just because you gave some scumbag credit. Because 'they seemed trustworthy'. And then you'll be a Deliveroo rider, *if* you can salvage ownership of a bicycle from the wreckage.

When I talk to other business owners it's the topic that reddens their angry glands like no other. Because a bad debt is, let's face it, stealing from you. There's so much wounded pride when you fall for the bait. The customer's plausible manner, your desperation to plug the revenue gap in a slow month, the lure of ongoing work from a shiny new client, then realising you've *paid them* for the privilege of working for them. You got shaken down like a country teenager who just got off a Greyhound bus in the big city.

Don't give anyone credit. Easy to say, harder to do, but a good place to start. Consider all the industries that wouldn't think of giving you credit. Supermarkets. Airlines. Hotels. Car dealers. Hospitals. Tattoo artists. You can tell them, 'I'm a business, I always get credit,' and they will say, 'Pay now or please leave our premises.'

Why should your business be any different? Giving people credit removes your only bargaining power: that they want something from you. After that, you're powerless. If they decide not to pay you, what are you going to do? You're going to consume a vast amount of your own valuable time, that's what. Placing calls they won't answer. Emails they 'didn't get'. Wasting all your time blows out the amount they're stealing from you. When you're angry, you're less productive, so it gets even worse.

The first law of credit is: the creditworthiness of a customer is inversely proportional to how aggressively they demand credit. When you hear 'Don't you know who I am?', 'I've been in this industry much longer than your business', 'All your competitors give me credit' and that sort of puffed-up chat, you're getting to know a future rogue debtor who will be even more of a dick when they're avoiding your collection calls.

Then it's all 'We can't pay you until our customer pays us'. And you know their customer already has. They've spent the cash.

The usual source of bad debts is salespeople granting credit because they really wanted to make the sale. You can't let that happen. In an SME the only person granting credit should be you. You can do all the credit checks you like but, like all references, they're hardly going to put you on to someone who'll say bad things. My friend with the asphalting business is addicted to the CreditorWatch website, which pings him updates of clients being taken to court and other interesting dirt. It is terrifying how often a client is plausible in person, then it turns out they are literally in liquidation, making their credit request a crime. Laws don't seem to bother these people at all.

Our general approach is: you get credit after trading with us reliably for a year. Or if we've known you personally for years and can vouch for your morality. It keeps the bad debts minimal. A lot of bad payers rely on credit timelines formed in ye olden days of commerce, when invoice processing involved months of literal rubber-stamping, then more weeks for the cheque to be 'in the mail'. Call their bluff.

No credit for you, scumbag

Now you can just get their credit card, PayPal or other payment details instantly. Convenient new payment systems launch every week. No corporate card? Make them put it on their personal card and they can handle the reimbursement battle. Your customer's internal processes are not your problem. We now live in a golden era of getting paid on the spot. Claim what's yours.

A MILLION BUCKS
IN MISTAKES

My old corporate job was a perfectly good gig. Autonomy. Fun projects. Lovely people. Reasonably well paid. I had done my Malcolm Gladwell-prescribed 10,000 hours of listening to people who wanted a quiet word about their troubles. It reached the point where someone would knock on the door of my pleasant corner office and I could tell purely from their facial expression what they wanted to talk about. I knew the answer before they sat down. I had everything covered, and faced no risks at all. I was bored out of my mind.

I needed higher highs and lower lows. That was the point where I knew I had to start my own business. Danger and pain make the pleasurable bits so much better, even if that mindset also killed Michael Hutchence.

Six months later, I lived for a week in a seedy $49-a-night Motel 6 with strong car park shootout vibes in Rancho Dominguez, a corner of Los Angeles next to Compton. I was pitching my marketing agency to a client in the area. I practised my pitch late into the evenings, breathing a halo of burnt fat particles from the Carl's Jr next door.

Damn, it was exhilarating. I won the client and it was an amazing feeling. To this day I enjoy American filter coffee when I'm in America, even though it tastes like a warthog's bath water. Because it takes me right back to that exhilarating tension of business missions to the Land of Freedom.

The peak of Success Mountain is a much nicer place if you've climbed up from some filthy ditch, and that expedition will involve stupid mistakes. Let's take a trawl through four of mine that each burnt over $100,000. In total, they're over $1 million. These figures aren't abstract sums we raised from venture capital. This was all our own cash, money we could have spent personally on, say, lobsters.

Buying a building like Mr Monopoly

We had a windfall profit in our Tasmanian business one year, and we thought: what would Mr Monopoly do? We bought our own office and warehouse. Within two years, we'd outgrown it and it was a massive brake on the business. We rented a twice-as-big space in the same complex. Right opposite our old place, so we could see the 'For Sale or Lease' sign fading as seasons rolled by with no enquiries.

It sat empty for two years until we sold it for a solid loss. Nice work, investment dabblers. Owning buildings limits your business to that space, and what's right now isn't right in the future. Our Sydney office has moved four times in twelve years and each was the right space at the right time. We could have kept that business as a nice goldfish. But with bigger bowls, and then ponds, it's grown into a handsome koi carp.

Also, if you can't earn a higher return on your capital from your business than from a building, you're not very good at business. The only reason to buy a building is if you're young and you expect your business to stay the same size forever. But it's a pretty unambitious outlook. Generally, the real returns come from doing what you're good at.

Coming to the attention of the Tax Office

One year we got on one of those magazine Top 50 Fast Growing lists. Not a bad achievement for a non-digital, high-capex business. It felt like we'd arrived. As we grew, we were being (we thought) prudent about our tax. A couple of the businesses around the country were nearly at a size where they'd have to pay payroll tax. We were ready.

Then I got a call from our accountant, saying the Tax Office had been in touch. Turns out, due to common shareholders, all our companies were classed as one business. We should already have been paying payroll tax. We should have started eighteen months ago.

We had a back-tax bill of $120,000. Due in a month. I have only yelled at people like a psychopath three times in the history of our business, and that was one of them. You had one job, accountant. Turns out it all came from a Tax Office guy in Tasmania reading the magazine list. Though we have nothing to hide, I'd avoid those lists. Ask your accountant what attracts Tax Office attention, like buying cars for cash. Don't do those things.

Ignoring the balance sheet

As an ad writer, you really learn your craft on boring products. It's easy to write a fun ad about tropical islands or beer. Harder to bring out the magic of professional indemnity insurance or tyres. Now I'm going for gold on the dull topic podium by talking up my favourite financial statements.

For years I was a Profit & Loss guy. That's the sexy-ass side of town, with its flashing scores lit up after the full-time siren, the proof you crave that you're way beyond last year's bonsai growth. Some months there are unexpected whuppings, but they make the glorious victories even sweeter. I ignored frumpy old Balance Sheet, like those periodic blood-screening tests you never quite get around to. They move so slowly, why bother checking? Then, because you weren't paying attention, some stony-faced professional informs you that you have a potentially terminal condition. Balance sheets speak the truth you may not want to hear.

We have had businesses go into the intensive care unit from stretching the balance sheet too tight. You're only one big tax bill or late customer payment away from trouble. You must learn to balance stock, capital assets, free cash, debts. A strong balance sheet got us through COVID-19, like a bear full of salmon with winter setting in. We had very little debt. The ribs were showing when we emerged from the COVID-19 cave, but that bear was breathing. I'm conscious you're bored already but this is so important. If your accountant can't explain it, get a new accountant.

Neglecting insurance broker emails

The TV news can be depressing sometimes. Like the night I saw a report of flash flooding on main-street Hobart. Cars floated by, then a shot from a tall building with a river of brown water gurgling down a car park ramp to create Hobart's newest indoor dam. The location seemed familiar. Ah yes. It was the building where our Hobart office is. And our warehouse full of expensive technology was *in that car park*. I called our local team. Yep, over a metre of putrid water had drowned our gear.

Half our stuff was elsewhere, but half a million dollars in high-tech equipment lay rotting in the swamp. That obviously sucked, but such is business. We were insured, whew. At claim time a person called a loss adjuster comes to survey the destruction and make sure it's legit. After two days of sniffing through slime-filled projectors, he pronounced it a valid claim. With a footnote: the policy needed individual assets listed. That list had not been updated for *four years*.

Most of the dead equipment wasn't on the insured list. Of the $500,000 damage, the approved payout was . . . $110,000. Taking the expression 'money down the drain' to the next level.

By coincidence our insurance broker, Tayla, is in Hobart. We've used her company for all our businesses nationally since we started, because Tasmanians are super-friendly and helpful. She went into battle with the insurance company like a warrior queen, on the grounds that we'd paid years of premiums on the full value. The insurer was absolutely within their rights to stick to the low payout. Anything extra was coming out of their pocket.

After three months, we settled on a payout of $420,000. Remember that earlier comment about building up brownie points with suppliers? There's the result right there. That insurance screw-up could easily have put our Tasmanian business six feet under, just from sloppy admin. Starting a business without proper insurance is like creating an essential document, updating it for five years, but never saving it once. You're only one kicked-out power cable or software crash away from losing everything because you were a disorganised fool.

Business insurance works through brokers. They work out what you need, and shop it around to find the best insurance company – the underwriter, in industry jargon. As a general rule, find a broker that knows your industry. They'll have a better idea of what risks you face. When they send you an email, read it. Or ye shall be smote by Old Testament biblical punishment, like us.

THE BUY-OUT: MEET YOUR NEW OVERLORDS

If you really insist on floating your business, you'll need to grow it up to adult size. If your business is a grower, private equity firms will 'reach out' with plans to 'unlock the value' in your firm. You visit their plush offices and admire the views and deluxe furniture. It's so much nicer than your own humble industrial park set-up and you think: I wouldn't mind a bit of this high-rolling business lifestyle. After all this brutal effort, I've earned it.

They know that's what you want. They paint a vivid picture of your dream life of boats, holiday houses and first-class trips to Tuscany. You want it so bad you let them creep the purchase price down and sneak in sinister terms like 'claw back' to reduce your payout when you fail to meet targets. You may not fully understand the details, but be under no illusion: any clause with the word 'claw' is not for your benefit.

It's much the same as old-school record contracts, where starry-eyed young bands got tied into contractual servitude with clauses making them pay for every over-budget video clip, record company sales junket, and executive 'fruit and flowers' (standard general ledger code for 'hookers and coke'). Not only was there no payoff for the band, five years later they'd break up owing the record company millions.

There might be private equity outfits out there that are honourable and want to help you build a great business. Just none of the ones we, or any of our friends, have been involved with. Once you sign the deal, you are hostage to a gang of ex-private schoolboys. They heap scorn on you and your staff for having no high-level business skills, even though those staff created the growth that made you worth buying. In the eyes of the finance lads your people have antiquated skills, equivalent to blacksmithing or apothecary. They get persecuted until they leave, and are replaced with MBAs.

Your new overlords will apply a terrifying range of charges and fees for their services that you don't fully understand. They will extract their purchase money from the business on about day three and ratchet up your debt to the point that if you were a developing nation, Bono would take up your cause.

All the time you used to spend looking after staff and clients you now spend filling out reports. Dozens per month. Writing reports is your new business model. Once a month, you have a board meeting where you get berated for your cautious financial projections because they want bigger, faster growth. They demand you add extra fees and charges, like a 'service fee' on every invoice, which will royally piss off your dedicated clients and drive them to your competitors.

You are a salaried prisoner in your own business for a minimum of the three years they like to hold you captive. All for a payout of three to four times your annual earnings. You could have kept the business and in a few years you would have had the same amount of money you got for the sale. Plus you would have had zero meetings with the private equity boys. Why did you even take the call from these tapeworms?

Now it's time for the debt-financed acquisition spree, where they snap up similar businesses with all the discerning caution of pro footballers on Mad Monday. Companies that were once sworn enemies are bought and clumped together around the board table like your worst Christmas dinner ever.

When we were under private equity ownership in our employee days, we would call business owners who had their act together, and try to buy them out. These were people with no debt, who had managers running the business for them, and worked in the business as much or little as they liked. They'd look at us and say: 'So you want me to surrender my freedom and become your employee bitch for three to four years' profit? Thank you, but no.'

Why wouldn't you just keep the business? Maybe you know it's secretly doomed by technical obsolescence, past its best, or it's some on-trend business like beard oil with a limited life. In which case, sell. These renovators' delights are the kinds of businesses that the private equiteers will add to yours, justified by mystical 'synergies' and 'back-office efficiencies' that are mostly fantasy.

In fact, your back-office costs are about to jack up alarmingly, as now you must use insanely expensive multinational accounting firms, auditors and lawyers. Lots of them, because the share-market gods must be appeased. You employ back-office battalions working on reports to be laid at the feet of pimpled junior analysts. Now that you're about to float, they hold powers of life and death over you like the impetuous teenage kings and queens of medieval times.

When you do float, the pressure to keep growing continues. There will also be pressure from the analysts about your own suitability to run the business. They view you as a corner-store manager who has arrived in this position by fluke and they would like you replaced with a proper career CEO. They will win this battle. You will be given a title like 'Executive Director, Special Projects' and they'll bring in a CEO whose last role was in waste disposal or some other unrelated field. Your successor is determined to put their stamp on the business, destroying the last shreds of what made it special. The debt levels escalate and you have grave doubts about how long this house of cards can hold up.

Lucky you sold out for cash instead of shares in the larger entity. What's that? You took the shares?

At this point I have that feeling you get when bigger kids have tricked your small child into paying $20 for a chocolate bar. You feel so sorry for them but that cash isn't coming back. Put it down to life lessons and your kid will get another $20 one day. But you? All your worldly wealth, the result of years of insane sacrifice, is now 100 per cent in the hands of egotists who don't fully understand what your company does. Whose only loyalty is to their next bonus.

You are so fucked.

I've known a few people who have sold their business for shares and the number who didn't get a royal rogering is zero. Payment in shares, or even cash and shares, is the oldest sideshow trick in the book. You've done so well to get your business to this point. Don't lose it all at the final turn. These people do not have your interests at heart. If you must sell, get the cash. Then all their petulant demands and misguided strategies are water off a duck's back. Don't spend it all. You might be able to buy everything back for a bargain in a few years.

8.

UNDISRUPTABLE: ESSENTIAL, TIMELESS SKILLS

SKILLS TECH CAN'T KILL

One reason business can be so exhausting is having to be on top of every new trend. There's so much late-night reading about what new social platform is tomorrow's killer marketing tool. Opinion leaders tell you strategies you once held dear are dead. The water around you churns with disruption piranhas. You want to know everything. Particularly if you, like me, fear irrelevance more than death itself.

You need this paranoia, but too much will fry your brain. A more productive approach is to hire people who can look after the tactics. While you handle the strategy, thinking and influence. The long-game art of business is finding people you can trust and giving them the freedom to do quality work. Then you can move up the food chain with timeless skills that aren't hostage to weekly changes in algorithms, viruses, tax rulings or meme spiciness.

Here are some essential, futureproof skills you can keep building through your whole career.

1. Look beyond your specialty skill

The ability to see things from outside your own specialty subject is essential if you're ever to get up the ladder. I loved being a creative

217

director a lot, and I could bore you for hours about fonts and colour grading. But I always knew business people didn't give a rat's about the details. As a business owner, I still love marketing, but it's just one thing among many. Meeting payroll for sixty-five people each month will turn any hipster aesthete into a cold-eyed, heartless merchant in quick time. When payables are way in excess of receivables, don't be telling me Helvetica is the answer.

A wider view also opens your eyes to new competitors. In our field, everyone loves events so much that they think a cool show is always the answer. The client might want to keep their workforce motivated for the rest of the year. Maybe those staff would be more motivated if everyone got a new luxury desk chair and a handwritten thank-you note from the CEO. If you asked that client different questions up front, you might realise you're competing against chairs. That needs a bigger-picture discussion than just 'Check out this awesome event design'.

2. Learn to follow the money

It's essential to be able to follow the money: who gets what as a result of the proposed plan, who approves the budgets, who owes favours to whom. Camouflage and red herrings abound. Without these detective skills, client behaviour is a mystery. Corporate decisions make no sense. No matter what your job, learn to read financial reports.

A sales director friend got an 80 per cent pay rise, which he appreciated. But he hadn't been doing much differently that year. He did some digging behind the scenes. Turns out the CEO was unhappy with his $700,000 package, and felt he deserved something a bit more seven-figure-y. So he brought in remuneration consultants, at a cost of $30,000. They told him that to get the million, he needed a lot more people under him on $250,000 or so. So he handed out raises like Halloween treats.

The more you follow the money trail, the easier it is to solve these mysteries. I've seen a department in a big company starved of funding they deserved, the cuts engineered behind the scenes by the CFO, because he saw the other department head as a future rival for the CEO position. During COVID-19, a global insurance company gave most of their workforce a 20 per cent pay cut, even though revenues were largely unaffected. Senior execs had their base salary cut 50 per cent. How very noble. Wait, look over there! The salary cuts boosted the company's bottom line, which kept that year's executive bonuses intact. So those senior execs were well ahead on the deal. It took a major industry outcry and the loss of key staff before they refunded the pay cuts.

If you feel someone is trying to screw you, this knowledge helps you understand their motives. If you're in a big company, befriend mid-ranking people in the finance department: they're usually well-placed to tell you what's really going on.

3. Be charming

Being charming takes the skill to spot when something is important to people, then be interested in it. It takes restraint most don't have. When someone tells you about the amazing video you should check out, must you tell them you already saw it? Rather than letting them feel like they're ahead of the curve?

If someone tells a story that's clearly a life highlight, like when they saw one of the lesser Hemsworths buying chicken wire at Bunnings, get excited for them. Do not mention that you once spilled a plate of mixed dips on a better Hemsworth in an airport lounge, and he was *so* charming about it. Conversation is not poker.

Remember this handy nineteenth-century British political anecdote. Jennie Jerome, who became Winston Churchill's mum, dined alongside Britain's Prime Minister William Gladstone one night, then the Opposition Leader Benjamin Disraeli the next. She wrote of the experience that after dining with Mr Gladstone, 'I thought he was the cleverest man in England. But when I sat next to Mr Disraeli, I thought I was the cleverest woman.'[7]

Disraeli beat Gladstone in the 1874 election. Be more Disraeli.

4. Be curious

The best thing about my ad-writing life was visiting clients and hearing about their new products and plans. It's such a positive cycle. You learn so much, plus they like you because you're interested in their work, unlike their own family. Also, I was always grateful for my own pleasant office after the visits. One multinational client had a rat trap every two metres down the office corridor.

When you're talking to other clients, you can bring ideas from one industry to another and look smarter than you are. If you're in the early part of your career and you haven't quite found your niche yet, take a job that's client-facing over one that isn't. The information you pick up builds, layer by layer, until you're a master of general business knowledge you can apply in any situation.

You won't get that if you're trapped in a closed-off department, where your only teacher is Vicki the office manager. It's a lifelong skill. The more you learn, the better questions you ask. Your conversations go to a higher level. Your value increases.

5. Learn to write better

I would say that, wouldn't I? It's true, though. Writing may be 5000 years old but it's an essential, scalable success tool right now. As things get more digital, so much of life is written rather than spoken. It remains the fastest, most accurate way to communicate, except in arguments. Yet most business people suck at it. Trying to find the core message in corporate memos and speeches is like trying to find a lost earring in a full vacuum cleaner bag.

The art is to get people's attention, get to the point fast, then stop. We've already covered how people will work with you if they like you. The best way to do that is in person, but you can only meet so many people each year. Write well and you can get an unlimited number of people to feel that they know and like you.

Writing can get you past the gatekeepers, now that nobody takes your phone call. It gives your staff a clear idea of what to do. Writing is much harder to dispute later. It's not all epic documents, either. The way you come across in every email, message or social post builds up like a coral reef over years to create your reputation.

People think pictures and videos are the future. They help, but they never close a deal. Video of people talking is a catastrophic time-waster. Write it down and people can read it in a quarter of the time. Pictures are good to attract attention, but for the vast majority of business, it's words that do the heavy lifting. Try winning a commercial contract with a picture book. Or building company culture. Try pitching for investors using photos only.

Writing is thinking. The act of writing your idea down clarifies it. How will it get interpreted when you're not there to explain? Anyone who does corporate sales pitches knows the horror of doing a compelling presentation to client middle management, then realising that it's up to *them* to pitch your precious message to their bosses. An idea that works on paper is stronger, clearer and stands a much better chance of surviving out there in the wild.

Read it aloud. It's a great test of whether it's good enough. I'll write my blog, then record the audio version and think: Did chimps break into my laptop overnight and tap this out? If it's important, it needs as much time editing as writing the first draft.

Copywriter habits infuse everything I write: emails, texts, social posts. The opening line has to get their attention or they're not going any further. The only place to start is: what's in it for the reader? We've won major tenders because we were the only ones who wrote something understandable with the benefits up front. There's money in writing.

6. Learn to apologise

You will fuck things up and be wrong on this journey. It's an essential part of the deal.

Learn to say 'I was wrong'. It's a strong, counterintuitive move. Saying 'You were right and I was wrong' to your staff makes them feel good, and shows you care about the end result more than petty point scoring. It will not diminish you in any way.

Same if you said or did something stupid. Most people use the non-apology format:

'I'm sorry if you were offended.'

Not good enough. Don't try to put the responsibility back onto them. Say something like:

'I'm sorry about what I said. It was out of line and I shouldn't have said it. Please accept my apologies.'

You build a lifetime reputation for taking responsibility like a grown-up. It stands out among the bosses who believe they can do no wrong.

BAD COP SKILLS:
AT LEAST BE A PRO

Part of what you are paid for is delivering bad news. You are not a store Santa. Things don't always work out happily ever after and you owe it to people to handle it like a pro. Not like 'Good news face to face, bad news by email' managers. It's a heavy situation to tell a business partner their dream is over. It's tempting to let it go another week or month, but when you know, you know. Do it as soon as possible.

When delivering bad news, get to the damn point. They know it's bad news. They can smell it. If you do a three-minute speech first, they're not listening. All they hear is an inner voice loop going 'Am I fired? Am I fired?' Just open with: 'There's no easy way to say this, but we don't have a job for you anymore.' Or whatever the bad news is.

Let them talk. If they want to yell at you, let them. Their concerns are bigger than yours right now. Their livelihood is gone, hopefully temporarily, and those concerns need addressing. Have all the numbers at hand: leave owed, redundancy payments and so on. You owe them as much certainty as you can provide.

Peter and I sometimes discuss the people we've let go over the years in our old jobs. It's hard to think of a case where that person wasn't better off in the long run. People shouldn't stay in jobs they're crap at. There will be something out there that suits them better. Bear this in mind when your inner voice says: 'I just ruined someone's life.' No, you didn't.

It's not only terminations. It's also about being open with people. That saved our business in 2020. Most businesses operate on a need-to-know basis, with management hoarding information like sales, profit or loss. We don't see the point of this. So we tell our staff pretty much everything. If the business is going well or badly they should know about it. They like this transparency.

As COVID-19 started to hit, events became illegal. We held all-staff meetings in each city. We told them that our whole industry was about to go over Niagara Falls in a barrel, and we couldn't predict exactly how things would end up. It had taken us a decade to assemble an *Avengers*-style super team, and we wanted to prove how much we value them.

We literally showed them our bank balance and books. And told them that though there was zero revenue, we would pay them to work three days a week until there was no money left, leaving enough to reopen one day. We had about six months. They were nervous about the future, but pleased to know where our priorities lay.

That week I wrote in my blog: *People will remember what you did this week for the next decade or more.* That same week, lots of other companies in our field pitched all their staff over the side, like some hideous slave ship incident.

Ten days later, the JobKeeper subsidy came in and those companies brought their staff back. Didn't matter; we all saw what they did back there. Ask those staff to 'go the extra mile' or whatever and they'll say: 'Sure.' They will not go an extra inch until the end of time. When those companies start hiring again, only the desperadoes will apply. Their downward spiral is locked in. Our staff remain a cheerful and united team.

NETWORKING
FOR INTROVERTS

I got described in an industry news story as a 'networking champion' and I only include that repellent, boastful-sounding item to balance out the far-from-champion truths that follow. I really like people, but I find regular networking a horrifying task. It's a subject that could use better guidance than you get from many networking experts. You see a lot of garbage advice in business and on top of that ibis-pecked dumpster are people who are *not* afraid of things telling people who *are*: 'Don't be afraid! There's *nothing to worry about.*'

Nothing except for their brain sending uncontrollable spasms of fear to block every attempt to do that thing. Advice from people who are really good at things can be surprisingly useless, because they've forgotten what it was like to *not* be able to do those things. Hence a lot of networking advice is confidence-jock boilerplate like:

- Just jump right in, what's the worst that can happen?
- Get out there and conquer your fears.
- Everyone else is just as uncomfortable as you.
- Each setback makes you stronger.

Whatever. It reminds me of sports coaching. I have pursued non-involvement in sport to an elite level. Every time I've tried to pick up

225

skills, the coach demonstrates how *they* can execute a move perfectly, then says: 'So do *that*! Just watch what I do!'

Mate, I can watch people do it perfectly on TV, so how about you break it down for people who fall backwards putting their shoes on. Same for the art of approaching a room of business strangers in full herd mode. Like most fears, Cocktail Banterphobia follows no logic, and it's weirdly selective. Conversations are my favourite thing. I like talking to cab drivers. I find presentations to any size audience curiously relaxing.

But rooms full of people I don't know fill me with evil dread every time. The barrier is purely about breaking into the circle of people, because what do I have to say that's better than the fascinating chat they're already having? I hate the thought of being that guy who barges in and drags the subject straight down to 'So, any plans for the weekend?'

Name recall is so difficult, yet so important. I take some pride in remembering the names of all our staff and most of their partners. It's essential to stop yourself turning into Creepy Visiting Boss who just nods at everyone. I put them in my phone contacts list and check the newest ones out on the flight beforehand.

At networking functions, though, you meet so many circular batches of six people, introduced by someone who has known them all for years. 'Ian, I'd like you to meet Dan, Amy, Susan, Ketan, Louise, Hema' – you try, but it's like having six tennis balls thrown at you at once. My unicorn idea is Shazam but for faces. Sometimes conversations start like:

Me (*enthusiastic and out to make a good impression*): Hi! I'm Ian!
Other Person (*disappointed face*): I know, we met last year, remember?
Me (*thinking*): *Fuck, I don't remember that at all.*

So I hit on a workaround: pretend I've met *everyone* before, so the ball's in their court.

Other Person: Hi, I'm Karen.
Me: Karen, great to see you again!
Karen (*who has never met me*): Oh, yes, of course. How've you been?

It's only failed once:

Me: Hi David, great to see you again!
David: No, we've never met.
Me: Uh.

None of this is going to help sales of my next book on power networking, is it? Here's a breakthrough networking 'hack' you won't find elsewhere. If you find networking functions an ordeal, *just don't go*.

Go somewhere else for a while. I got to know most of the people in my industry in small meeting rooms by volunteering for the industry association board. Through that I've made lots of lovely friends who are scattered around each cocktail party, so now I can swan up to groups like the Mayor of Networkville and say hi in born-to-do-it style. Pure illusion.

If I didn't know those people, I'd be hiding in my hotel room eating club sandwiches. Join industry committees and working groups or anywhere you've got something to do, rather than just standing around talking yourself up.

If you're in the early years of your career, the people you meet this way will randomly pop up decades later and give you the inside running on some tender or job opportunity, so you're not forever condemned to wander the barren wastelands of the level playing field.

HOLIDAYS: A TEST OF YOUR BUSINESS SKILL

I can tell how good you are at business by your holiday skills. Seems strange, maybe, but stay with me. When you start a new business, you never take a break because holidays are for the weak. You can survive three or four years of this sergeant-major mindset, because hard work never killed anyone, especially when you're young. But it catches up with you. What's that line people always roll out? Nobody ever looked back on their deathbed and wished they'd spent more time at work?

Not sure about that one. You could also look back on your deathbed and consider the great education and opportunities your children had because your hard work allowed that to happen. Plus you helped lots of employees build worthy careers, and you got to do a ton of interesting, fulfilling stuff yourself because you could afford it. Watch less Netflix, do the work and your deathbed arrangements will look after themselves.

If you've been in business more than four years and you take no holidays, you have a low-quality business, which isn't going to get any bigger or better, and you have poor delegation skills. If you take at least one annual holiday where you only contact work once a week or so, you are well-organised and your business is a success.

Holidays

Why so? Holidays force you to sort out your growth obstacles. If you can't trust people to run the business while you're away, you need to take a hard look at your paranoid mindset. The whole point of a business is to employ people to do things, rather than doing it all yourself. If none of your current staff are up to running the place for a few weeks, you need better staff.

If you can't afford to hire better staff to cover for you, you need to lift your prices or change your revenue model. If you're the only one who knows the processes that run the business, your cat-lady hoarder mentality will keep your business capped at its current size forever. The act of being able to take a holiday shows you're on top of the issues that will allow your business to grow.

It's a great opportunity for your staff to lift. How are they going to learn and show their skills if you never give them the chance to rise above their current gig? If they do a great job . . . great. You're on your way to better succession planning. Worst-case scenario and they do a bad job, you know more about those staff than you did before. *And* you had a holiday.

If you never take a break, your brain shrinks down to a mental shoebox filled with receipts. Cruelly, that brain tricks you into thinking you're doing a great job holding everything together in that special way *only you can do* because you are the star of your own business action-hero movie. Only you can take down Hans Gruber and save Christmas for everyone.

In fact, your business is plateauing at best. Your energy is at iPhone-at-4pm levels, and your only source of inspiration is your lunchtime trip to Subway. You're just like every other water-treading business martyr.

Ideas come to you when you're doing nothing. Great ideas can be stolen from other industries, in other places. You don't need to move to Cuba or hit the absinthe, but you will need to leave the office. All the business owners I know come back from holidays pulsating with energy and ideas, desperate to return and get some cool shit happening.

Vacation starvation is bad for your brain and kills any ability to think outside the spreadsheet. China has five days of annual leave in the first ten years of your job. That's one reason why their whole economy is making cheaper versions of ideas thought up by people in countries that offer staff a decent break. Unless your business is cheap offshore manufacturing, your future depends on out-thinking competitors. Recharge that brain annually or else.

THE CURE FOR RESTING
BASTARD FACE

Want to be happier, help your business life *and* look good later in life without injectables? Practise being a decent person at all times, not just when it suits your greedy needs. So many people are charming to clients, and also happy to throw staff and suppliers under the bus. They have a deep need to have someone to pick on, a big neon indicator of their own insecurity. They love a bcc email: they 'just thought you should know'. Most of all, they love this joke structure:

1. Some gross insult
2. A pause, then . . .
3. 'Just joking!' and a wink and shoulder pat.

People who do this 100 per cent mean that insult literally, and think they're getting away with it in the same way people say 'No offence, but . . .' Good humour punches up, not down, and so does good management. Good managers will take a fight to those above them, to defend their staff from stupidity and persecution.

Punching down is so weak. I have an incandescent loathing of radio prank calls to businesses. Radio jocks calling up to humiliate a front-desk service worker or store salesperson. Nice work, anonymous tough guys. That shop assistant totally fell for your hilarious lines and how confused and stupid did they sound ha ha ha!

That's not comedy, that's abuse. A smirking radio team on six-figure salaries harassing someone on $16.20 an hour. Store staff have no choice but to take that stupid banter at face value. Because every day, real customers make requests just as insane. What if they told those callers to fuck off and stop wasting their time? They'd lose their job on the spot. Would you be willing to lose your job to give Jacko, Jimbo and Becky from The Morning Menagerie three minutes of on-air material? I wouldn't either. That sort of entertainment comes from the same mindset as making bears dance on hotplates.

Now consider your own treatment of phone salespeople. Obviously, their work is annoying. Since *Seinfeld*, comedians have built routines out of torture techniques for sales callers who dared to interrupt their dinner. So most people feel they can treat them like garbage. You hear them telling the story.

'Ha ha, those sales callers, I asked them to go on hold, made 'em wait five minutes, got back on and told them to get fucked.' Everyone says: 'Good one, they deserved it.'

Step back and consider who you're punishing. It's the battling single parent who can't work any other job because of the kid time constraints. It's the student with no family financial support, trying to scrape up rent for the apartment they share with eight others. They're working under the worst conditions you can imagine. If you think humiliating them is cool, you should consider what that says about you.

But what about if they have a foreign accent, the number one screening factor for most people? You feel less guilt about insulting those guys, right? Okay, so you're saying that they're somehow less deserving of human respect purely because you can't quite understand them over a crappy phone line. Because they're not the well-spoken person from your own race you'd prefer to be selling you mobile data packages.

That's quite the 1960s South African country club mindset, isn't it? Also, they can speak English. How are your foreign language skills, champ?

I'm not saying buy their stuff just to be nice. Odds are you don't want it, and it's a broken, annoying sales medium. But if you're pissed off at the Relentless Interruption business model, call that company's CEO and let them have it. They won't take your call. But don't take it out on the boiler room people. All it takes is a polite 'Thanks, I don't want to waste your time, I'm not interested.' That's all.

Don't get me wrong, I'm no Jesus of polite restraint. There reaches a point, thirty minutes into a phone call that is always about internet faults, where I lose it at the sheer goldfish experience of telling the same story to four consecutive people, and become a much worse version of myself. It spoils the next two or three hours because you're pulsing with anger chemicals that make you unproductive.

Why is this trivial behavioural adjustment important? Because you're forming a micro-habit of treating everyone with respect. Perhaps even considering how their lives are different to yours. It will change how you relate to your staff and your clients. Being reasonable to everyone stops you peppering your day with doses of microaggression. You don't notice it because it's a drip-feed change, but each little flare-up makes you less happy. Later in life, it will turn you into one of those people who writes long get-off-my-lawn letters to the council and local media.

People can see you doing the nice-to-some routine, so you create a lifelong rat reputation. Play it straight and you'll win clients years later, because you were decent to a random person and they remembered. I can tell if you're a good or bad person purely by whether you're decent to service staff. As the saying goes in the dating world, watch how people treat waiters, because that's how they'll be treating you in six months.

Business really is a better experience if you get on with all of your staff, and don't act like they should feel blessed by your godlike presence. If you're a dick, that behaviour gets green-lighted right through your organisation and then you've built a total dick brand.

If you're a boss you might only see some of your staff for a few minutes once a year. You've had a terrible week dealing with all sorts of evil, you're hyper-stressed and your mind is elsewhere. It's so easy to be offhanded like you're super-important and they are mere serfs. Yet their entire impression of you is based on these few moments. You need to summon up the energy and focus on them.

If you've been practising being decent to service staff and phone salespeople, it's second nature to you. It's pure muscle memory. It's also important because for your business to be a success, you will have to ask people to do unreasonable things. They'll do it if they respect you.

If you let microaggression infest your life it will literally set into your face. John the photographer and I did a lot of annual reports and law websites. That meant lots of portrait shoots of older finance and law people. You could tell their inner character within ten seconds of pre-shot banter.

Most were lovely. Then there were the ones whose faces had been shaped by a full working life of ill-temper and adversarial attitude. Bulldog jowls. Lower teeth slightly jutting out and brows knotted in a permanent scowl. You'd ask them to smile and they physically couldn't. We had a specific Photoshop tool to make them a bit less terrifying, a sort of flesh spatula.

Resting bastard face is real. Don't end up there, terrifying your own grandchildren.

STAY CLASSY: TEN TIPS FOR BUSINESS DRINKING

A lot of tiresome media advice appears each November on how to survive Christmas party season. Each story has quotes from pursed-lipped office managers who want you to party like they would (i.e. in a way that is not any kind of party).

This is not realistic. I've done diligent tests of the corporate party environment, and found it to be both fun and a productive business strategy. Like most useful skills, being able to drink alcohol at business events while remaining pleasant and fun to be around takes knowledge and effort. Some handy guidelines:

1. Spare us your smug charity clarity

Oh, so you're off alcohol for a month? You're doing Puritanuary, Feb-fast, Parched March, Abstain-pril, Moderation May, Judicious June, Dry July, No More-gust, Sensible-tember, Ocsober, Just Say No-vember, Detox-cember or any other of the endless pleasure-denial festivals inflicted on us by preachy health professional groups.

Sure, do it to support charity but please keep it to yourself. None of us care how clear-headed and mindful you feel. I much prefer the company of an honest, just-don't-like-alcohol or religious-reasons non-drinker over the month-off martyrs. You have a perfect right not to drink alcohol, and the competent drinker respects people who don't. Why does it matter if people are not drinking when you are? They don't owe you an explanation.

I really like alcohol, but not during the day. It makes me sluggish. So I worked out a simple barbecue technique. Have one beer in a green or brown bottle, then sneak into the laundry and refill it with tap water for the rest of the afternoon. Much easier than answering the endless loop of that same question about why I'm not drinking. As people get drunker, the braying sound of them wanting you to have *juuuust oooonnne* gets really tiresome. Be better than that.

2. Listen to the inner voices

Moderate alcohol speeds up almost all essential business processes, lowering the walls of cowardice and indecision – yours and others' – that block progress. Clients tell you what they really think. Decisions you agonise over in daylight can seem really clear when your inner honest voices are let off the chain. You learn the deep-down natures of your staff much faster.

You should not sign documents or make irrevocable decisions when you are drinking, but don't discount your thoughts at these times.

3. Know your Latin

The Romans had all this down thousands of years ago with the expression *in vino veritas*, which our in-house Latin scholars translate to:

If you are, at your very core, a dickhead, you can hide it quite well during office hours, just as serial killers aren't always killing people. But get a few glasses of cheap catering wine under the belt, and it's cape on and take-off time for Super Dickhead, coming to save us all from a pleasant night out.

236

When people describe someone as a mean drunk or a morose drunk, in reality they're a mean or morose person who manages to hide it most of the time. If people are happy drunks, you know they're essentially a decent person.

4. Broaden your conversation base

Ninja business drinking skill is being able to listen to an evening of random jabbering and remember it all, so you can recall it next time you see that person in six months. Or being able, the next morning, to email them the link to that thing they found so interesting the night before. It's a handier business skill than Excel, and an essential factor in the growth of our own brand.

Alcohol should encourage you to broaden your conversation topics and the people you converse with. I'm lucky enough to work in an industry with a majority of women, and the conversation topics are so much wider and better. There's nothing worse than that musky blokes-club vibe of drunk guys in a closed circle, talking about nothing but work and footy. Embrace the chance to learn some new material.

5. Raise your bar budget, lower your meeting room budget

Early on, I knew Peter and I would start a business together one day, purely because we both have some kind of lucky enzyme mix that means we don't get hangovers.

So we're out there late at night at industry events, not drunk but professionally relaxed, taking it all in like information super-trawlers. You suck up a lot of verbal plankton and krill, which we're good with, as we genuinely love talking to people, and every so often you land some exotic fact that will be worth a lot to you. That might be in five years' time, but it's all stored away. Business is all about information, and you won't find the valuable stuff sitting at home scrolling through LinkedIn.

We're able to strike handshake deals in dark bars at 3 am, when people are stripped of their corporate veneer and able to express their feelings. I'm pretty sure we've never made any significant deals, sales or high-level hirings in offices or meeting rooms. I find them as stiff and artificial as any focus group.

6. If you can't drink, just don't

Lack of alcohol skills is a harsh litmus test. Over the years, in other businesses, we've had to whack salespeople who were mostly charming and were perfectly employable in every way but one.

They'd go to an industry dinner, be a jabbering munter an hour in, unleash the kind of jokes that end with '. . . just one goat!', touch clients with their wandering monkey paws, and create the sort of spectacle that brings awkward client emails the next day.

You can't have that stigma attached to your business. It hasn't been okay for decades, and the last few years have hammered home that reality. If you are one of these people, you can't drink when you're on company duty. There's no safe dosage, because once Super Dickhead gets the slightest taste, the inner voices say, 'Just one more, you'll be fiiiine.'

If you're a party dickhead, you aren't just ruining the good vibe on one night. You're making life worse for everybody over the long term. Internal killjoy departments are trying to regulate parties out of existence, and it's *because of you*.

Ask a range of your friends: Am I *that person* when we have more than a few drinks? If even one of them looks you in the eye and says yes, or even hesitates before they say no . . . it's permanent detox time for you, at least for your business life.

7. Get qualifications

Okay it's not a qualification that currently exists, but if any training institution wants to set up a CBD (Certified Business Drinker) diploma I'm up for helping with course development.

Candidates would get a benchmark level of drinks over three hours, while mingling in a business crowd. If they don't get handsy, show anyone a tattoo that would normally be covered at the beach, send self-pitying messages to their ex, or impersonate any kind of foreign accent, they'll have passed Part 1.

Part 2 is showing up for work the next morning on time, fully functioning and not reeking of cigarettes and kebabs. If you can't do that, don't drink. CBD graduates are qualified to go to social events, claim expenses and generally represent the business in Loose Situations in a way that builds long-term goodwill.

An essential part of that goodwill is being aware of what's going on around you. Scan the room for people who need rescuing from creeps and bores. Introduce people who can help each other. Keep an eye out for amateur drinkers who have gone in too deep, and get them a cab.

8. Drunk sales patter is the worst

For the PhD qualification, you have to navigate the CBD test without once mentioning your business and its leading-edge range of solutions. To do this, you must be interesting and, more importantly, interested in other people. It's one of the tragedies of the middle-aged professional that many lose the ability to talk about anything except their own tedious profession. So lawyers will cluster and talk all night about who will be made a judge and so forth. Fine if it's a gathering of lawyers at a Law Society cocktail party. But if there are regular citizens present, your mono-topic banter is charmless.

9. Invest time in future you

Only about 10 per cent of the grand plans and promises made in these late-night situations actually become a reality. That's still a better strike rate than daytime brainstorming with sandwiches and a facilitator. People may not wake up with specific knowledge of anything that was said but they still have a general feeling that you are likeable and can be trusted.

It's exactly like developing a brand. Feelings and instinct beat facts and logic every time. It's a long game, forming experiences that can bond you for life and creating business relationships that no standard meeting or sales call can ever do. The commercial returns are hard to justify on a single year's evaluation.

If you're in your twenties, the cocktails and after-parties you don't attend are costing Future You access to the secret club where stuff gets done offline, once your friends achieve power.

A business-dynamo friend with small kids pointed out that this reality holds a lot of women her age back, career-wise. She dreams of getting among the refreshments and talking shit with her peers till late at night, but it's a nightmare to plan. Partners: time to step up and mind those kids while the mother of your children gets to that conference or awards night. Outsiders think it's just a party. It's not, it's an essential career move.

10. Pick up the tab

There's a super-complex set of scales and balances around who pays the bill. Is someone a potential client? Who in the group works for a big company with lax expense approval processes? Who's having a hard year and deserves a free drink? You can't pick up the tab all the time, but you all know someone who is a chronic shout-evader.

They think they're getting away with it, as they order their usual deluxe cocktail and talk up how you'll be doing business together real soon. They make a show of pulling out the wallet or purse, waving it around with zero intent of opening it.

Everyone knows what they're up to. When the day of reckoning comes, they shall be judged by the all-seeing Etiquette God and cast into a vast cauldron of boiling pump-pack hot dog cheese.

Don't be that person. You're better than that.

STAY BUSINESS-FIT IN THE GYMNASIUM OF IRRITATION

Your own business puts insane demands on your time. You have to delegate hard. You need help for all those tasks that steal precious minutes from productive work. Airport bookshelves offer endless advice to manage your valuable time: get someone else to answer your emails, do your laundry and walk your dog. App stores are packed with exciting disruptive tools to bid these tasks out to a new underclass of helpers.

Plus as you get more successful you treat yourself to the little luxuries that a busy business person deserves for all that arse-busting effort, like the limo to and from the airport, and fair enough too. And yet . . . those nice things will also make you worse at what you do.

All the good business people I know are interested in the little everyday problems they encounter, and in coming up with ideas to solve them, even if it's just as a mental exercise. Daily life is a gymnasium of irritations large and small. Finding all the traffic lights in those shitty website are-you-a-robot tests. Delivery people who decide you're not home without knocking and take the parcel back to a warehouse in Broome. Cost comparison websites that find you the 'best' deal, then follow up with phone harassment worthy of a court restraining order. It's endless.

Better business comes from smart people going: *This is shit, I'm going to find a way to fix it.* If you palm every personal and business irritation off to people paid much less than you, you're now way out of touch with most of your customers, and the human race in general.

All your problems are smoothed out. Your queue is shorter. You don't mix with people who aren't like you. You don't know what really matters to regular folk, so it's much harder for you to recognise genuine opportunities. You lose your instincts for normal human behaviour, and that's the single most important skill in business. In your world of convenience, nobody would wait outside a store in the cold for hours to buy half-price bed linen. They wouldn't buy a bottle of wine for under $30. Your lack of reality calibration shows in all the little decisions you make on pricing and marketing messages, and in your mental images of who your customers are.

Gradually your idea of the real world shrinks to reflect the circle of people in your office, ashtanga yoga class or yacht squadron. You can't understand people worse off than you if your only contact with them is when they park your car. Understanding and insight come from talking to people. More than from the 'Female 25–39 AB Family-Oriented Life-style Seeker' stereotypes your marketing department serves up, claiming it's a breakthrough in behaviour prophecy. Their predictive caricatures are right sometimes. And so is astrology.

You lose touch with your staff. Because commuting presents no problems for you, you move your premises away from public transport and now your people pay twice as much to get to work. You make casual shifts shorter and now it costs them more in childcare than they're earning. You have no understanding of how hard their life can be as they battle to make ends meet. So working for you becomes . . . just another job.

When you have kids, delegation can free up precious time with them. But if you have your team of app-sourced servants do all the crappy jobs, your kids grow up seeing that as normal, and that makes them more likely to become Donald Trump Jr. So if your kid ends up shooting giraffes, don't say you weren't warned. And if you delegate all your dog walking to a dog walker, you don't deserve a dog.

You don't have to do it every day, but cook your own food. Go to the supermarket. Assemble your bookshelves. If Edison had a low-priced team of candle trimmers and oil-lamp refillers coming around to his house every day, he wouldn't have bothered inventing the light globe. Embrace everyday annoyance, your new inspirational friend.

HOW TO SUCCEED IN
SIXTY-FOUR WORDS

Puts on LinkedIn video voice Do you want *the secrets of success*?
Better still, do you want to *never have to go to success seminars*?
I'd call that a win. I don't want to curb your urge for self-improvement, but you can find better role models than the people who run those things. The hustle flourishes in hard times as the grifters sniff opportunity. They use techniques pioneered by history's top dictators to juice up loyal footsoldiers. Which helps if your job is standing in an airport terminal all day asking passers-by if they want wine subscriptions or credit cards. You can't be questioning the mission in gigs like that.

I know some pretty successful people, worth lots of money, if that's how you want to measure it, and none of them did the seminars. Not even when they were starting out. Most of them just read a lot and asked people lots of questions.

I'm no Tony Robbins, nor have I founded a unicorn. But I can suggest a list of eight not-so-difficult things that will ensure you become successful. You're not going to read them and go: 'Whoa! Genius breakthrough thinking!' They're all quite obvious, pedestrian tips. That's why most people don't do them. Here you go:

Eight low-key steps to success

1. Turn up on time.
2. Do the things you said you would do.
3. Be genuinely interested in people and in what they're doing.
4. Listen rather than talking over people.
5. Look for good ideas outside your own industry and steal them.
6. Mentally picture stuff you want to achieve.
7. Treat people like you want to be treated yourself.
8. Define success on your own terms, not other people's.

That's. It.

You can go to work now.

Those eight points are simple. Yet people want to believe that success is more complicated than it is. They're looking for the secret winning edge, the 1 per cent advantage over others. So they turn to neuro-linguistic programming or Lean Six Sigma, whatever those things are.

Their focus on the 1 per cent means they forget the 99 per cent, because basics don't carry that prestigious aura of expertise.

If you can do these basic things every day, you will succeed. If you can get your staff to do them consistently, they will sweep all competition before them. Honestly, you can just take action on this chapter and treat the rest of the book as light in-flight amusement.

I really hope you do start a business, if you want to.

And if it doesn't make a fortune, cool. Life is still great. Having a limitless source of instant clean water right there in your kitchen is luxurious. Living in a country where you can look out the window and see a kookaburra is a privilege. You can pop down to the shops whenever you like without worrying about car bombs. Raising kids well is a greater achievement than any business, and needs no investors. Use your freedom wisely.

NOTES

1. Lecher, Colin, 'How Amazon automatically tracks and fires warehouse workers for "productivity"', *The Verge*, 25 April 2019.
2. The Venture Podcast with Lambros Photios, 'Shark Tank Investor: This is How You'll Impress Me', Nov 2019, lambrosphotios.com/podcast/shark-tank-investor-this-is-how-youll-impress-me/.
3. Porsche, Twitter, 7 October 2016; twitter.com/Porsche/status/784121659494137856.
4. Stevenson, Seth, 'We're No. 2! We're No. 2!', *Slate*, 21 August 2013.
5. The State of LinkedIn, Twitter, twitter.com/StateOfLinkedIn.
6. This concept originally appeared and was attributed to General Kurt von Hammerstein-Equord in a UK periodical called 'Army, Navy and Air Force Gazette' in 1933: *Quote Investigator*, quoteinvestigator.com/2014/02/28/clever-lazy/#return-note-8291-1.
7. Marquand, David, 'The Charisma Question: Disraeli and Gladstone Reappraised', *New Statesman*, 25 July 2013.

ACKNOWLEDGEMENTS

I read this in a business magazine from a 'serial entrepreneur':

And finally …

I've learnt – the hard way – the perils of having a business partner. There's nothing worse than having to deal with money when you split a partnership. That's when people's true values surface.

I will never have another business partner again.

Employ everyone, or give them an incentive to be in your business. Keep control.

And I thought: Fuck, what a sad, suspicious life.

My business life has been an ongoing delight, all thanks to my Scene Change partners Peter, Vicken, Dinhgo, Gareth, Andrew and Badger. Your 'true values surfaced' and that's the whole reason the business works like it does. It's an honour, and unending entertainment, to work with you all. Control is overrated.

To Madeleine, Declan and Lacey for the intergenerational manuscript audit. Lacey also for the blog referral that got this show on the road.

To Fionn and James, the blog (and beyond) legal panel.

To Lachlan for the travel translations.

To Lambros and Dayne for the podcast fun.

Acknowledgements

To Rob, for the pub bet on who could be the first to write a book. You owe me one beer, sir.

To Izzy at Penguin Random House for providing literally the only good news I got for a whole year, without which I might have turned to absinthe addiction, or become one of those sad beach metal detector guys. Thanks to you and Kalhari for bringing the stories into focus and not forcing me to use correct words every time, like 'whom'.

And to Michelle for endless encouragement and invaluable advice when it seemed like all the effort was going nowhere for years. Love has many dimensions, and I love you in all of them.

Discover a
new favourite